Bill Downey, the author
of *Uncle Sam Must Be Losing the War,*
Black Viking, and
Tom Bass: Black Horseman,
is an instructor at Santa Barbara City College
in California. He teaches creative writing
and "right brain" writing courses.

Bill Downey

RIGHT BRAIN... WRITE ON!

Overcoming Writer's Block and Achieving Your Creative Potential

A SPECTRUM BOOK

PRENTICE-HALL, INC., Englewood Cliffs, New Jersey 07632

Library of Congress Cataloging in Publication Data

Downey, Bill.
    Right brain—write on!

    "A Spectrum Book."
    Includes index.
        1. Writer's block.   2. Creation (Literary, artistic,
etc.)   3. Creative writing (Higher education)
4. Authors, American—20th century—Interviews.
5. Cerebral dominance.   I. Title.
PN171.W74D68 1984   808'.001'9   83-27050
ISBN 0-13-780990-5
ISBN 0-13-780982-4 (pbk.)

1   2   3   4   5   6   7   8   9   10

ISBN 0-13-780990-5

ISBN 0-13-780982-4 {PBK.}

Editorial/production supervision: Marlys Lehmann
Cover design: Donna Bonavita
Manufacturing buyer: Pat Mahoney

This book is available at a special discount when ordered in
bulk quantities. Contact Prentice-Hall, Inc., General
Publishing Division, Special Sales, Englewood Cliffs, N.J. 07632.

Prentice-Hall International, Inc., *London*
Prentice-Hall of Australia Pty. Limited, *Sydney*
Prentice-Hall Canada Inc., *Toronto*
Prentice-Hall of India Private Limited, *New Delhi*
Prentice-Hall of Japan, Inc., *Tokyo*
Prentice-Hall of Southeast Asia Pte. Ltd., *Singapore*
Whitehall Books Limited, *Wellington, New Zealand*
Editora Prentice-Hall do Brasil Ltda., *Rio de Janeiro*

To EVALYN STAFFORD,
for her years of love and support
of writers and writing.

To AUNTIE SIS,
for her love and support.

CONTENTS

Preface *ix*
Acknowledgments *x*
Introduction *xiii*

1 **Our Right Brain Potential** *1*

2 **Making the Shift** *19*

3 **Trusting Your Writing** *36*

4 **Right Brain Exercise** *55*

5 **Enter the Editor: Left Brain** *73*

6 **Telling the Story** *92*

7 **Writing: The Holistic Approach** *106*

8 **Writing Assignments** *121*

9 **Research** *134*

10 **Writers Discuss the Block** *145*

Ted Berkman *147/*   William Manchester *151/*
Anita Clay Kornfeld *155/*   Charles Schulz *157/*
Saul Bellow *160/*   Irving Wallace *162/*   John Leggett *165/*
Barnaby Conrad *168/*   Susan Strasberg *171/*
Jack Smith *175/*   Budd Schulberg *178/*
Christopher Isherwood *182/*
Fannie Flagg *186/*   Art Buchwald *189/*
Alex Haley *191/*   Artie Shaw *195/*   Margaret Millar *198/*

Conclusion *205*
Index *207*

PREFACE

This book was born in a Santa Barbara adult education class listed as "Write On." The goals were to overcome writer's block and the creative lag that hounds writers at all levels. Two years later Betty Edwards wrote *Drawing on the Right Side of the Brain,* which became our only textbook. The Edwards book was for artists who wanted to improve their line drawing. But the author made it clear that the energy that flowed from the right brain for artists worked for writers as well.

I had expressed my interest in right brain perception to one of the adult education programmers, who immediately said that it must become a class. My background at the time included ten years as a newspaper reporter and columnist, two books, and many magazine assignments.

We decided that the classes would have to be radically different from other writing groups. Creativity must come first and academics a distant second. There had to be reasons why some writers have more access to creativity than others. From what had been learned at that time, it seemed apparent that we all have creativity, but some of us have greater access to it than others. So this would be our goal: learning to establish access to our right brain capability.

The first class was a very broad slice of the community. We had several teachers, one of them retired; a former assistant secretary of defense; a dentist; a doctor, and two nurses. Homemakers, professionals, and tradesmen made up the balance.

Our ground rules provided no tolerance for the heavy criticism normally found in this sort of class. Protection and assurance were guaranteed, and the observations made were supportive and positive. Yes, we nurtured the good and smothered the errors by denying them energy.

As a newspaper reporter I had learned long ago that every strike of the typewriter is not a gemstone. Everyone can stumble along the way. So why should a writer struggling for creative expression be peppered with critical ruler smacks? Our carefully sustained hothouse atmosphere was accepted without question. Each of us sought to establish and enhance our creative proficiency. There was encouragement; the group was nonthreatening. And it worked.

After a couple of sessions we were a family. The atmosphere was such that a poetry teacher heard about us and came to use our "good vibes" to grade her homework papers. By then the shy members were speaking out; the more aggressive ones were finding less need to be assertive.

An engineer with a block for writing technical papers found the answers to his dilemma—along with a bonus. In addition to renewing his old technique, he found himself writing lyric poetry. The divisions between fiction and nonfiction were forgotten, because each requires the elements of creativity that come of right brain thinking. Where is it written, we decided, that serious writing need be dull to be credible?

When the first session ended, we conducted an informal poll to find what single most important factor had been established. To our surprise, the most predominant item was: Writing can be fun. The sensation of pleasure, we found, derives of the right brain and helps to establish that mode.

A further surprise was the grandmother who said, "I might never be published. But thanks to these classes I rarely see my therapist more often than every sixty days." The therapeutic value of right brain perception is very real, but such had not been our original intent. Still, there is a message to consider: Writing has something for everybody.

Acknowledgments

This book could not have been completed without the scholarship, support, and inspiration of more persons than this page can list. My wife, Kim, shared in the creative development of this project and worked diligently for its completion. My son Michael was involved long before the first class was formed and his counseling skills were invaluable in forming a concept. My two youngest, Wayne and Leslie, waited as though a new baby were being born. Barnaby Conrad and Mary Conrad were both extremely generous with research and inside information—I am indebted to them. Anne Lowenkopf shared indexing skills at a most critical time, and Bill Adams made miracles happen with his photocopier. Anne Wooldridge found several important volumes of research in her personal library. The nuns of the Sarada Convent provided welcome sanctuary at the Vedanta Temple. And I do appreciate the wisdom and experience of the Prentice-Hall staff: Dennis Fawcett, Marlys Lehmann, and Jeanne Kramer. My writing classes over the past eight years have been a willing catalyst for the theories and techniques that are now established. And certainly not least in importance are the Santa Barbara librarians who contributed in their quiet, efficient way to this book and my previous four. To all of you and especially those who inadvertantly have been omitted here, I am grateful.

Grateful acknowledgment is also made for the use of:

Effective Writing, by Robert Hamilton Moore. Copyright © 1955 by Robert Hamilton Moore. Reprinted by permission of Holt, Rinehart and Winston, CBS College Publishing.

Journal of American Indian Education, Arizona State University. Spring 1983. Permission for quotations by the editor.

Max Perkins, Editor of Genius, by A. Scott Berg. Copyright © 1978 by A. Scott Berg. Reprinted by permission of E. P. Dutton.

Conceptual Blockbusting, by James L. Adams. Copyright © 1980 by James L. Adams. Reprinted by permission of W. W. Norton and Co. Inc.

American Tongue and Cheek, by Jim Quinn. Copyright © 1980 by Jim Quinn. Reprinted by permission of Pantheon Books, a Division of Random House, Inc.

Drawing on the Right Side of the Brain, by Betty Edwards. Copyright © 1979 by Betty Edwards. Reprinted by permission of J. P. Tarcher, Inc., and Houghton Mifflin Co.

A Practical Guide to Holistic Health, by Swami Rama. Copyright © 1980 by Swami Rama. Reprinted by permission of The Himalayan International Institute.

INTRODUCTION

Right Brain . . . Write On! is not a book, it's a writer's survival kit. It shows by example and experience that writers do not lose their grasp, they lose their direction.

For journeymen at all levels who have lost their compass heading, here is help—a navigational directory simplifying a course for more effective writing. The resolution of writer's block and creative lag are confronted from the working writer's point of view and not that of the theoretician.

No one will confuse this work with an intellectual treatise by some learned cornerstone. It has been written by a working writer whose newspaper/free-lance background has been used to help other writers. The deadline writer and newcomer both can find solid directions here.

The intellectual approach to writing has too many rules and restrictions coupled to a hidebound rigidity that does little to serve the needs of today's free-lancer. This is because rules and restrictions inhibit creativity, which is the lifeblood of the independent writer.

These pages will show quite early that in order to survive, writers at all levels must constantly come up with new and innovative material. The energy drain is substantial, and the writer instinctively turns to outside sources for reassurance. When none is forthcoming, the writer is afloat in the doldrums of nonproductivity. In desperation, authors have turned to radical and dangerous solutions. This need not be.

A source of energy greater than any other is available for floundering writers. The source originates from within. Solid directions through right brain perception can provide answers for those whose creativity seems lost, whose production seems blocked.

In a sacred manner they are sending voices.
Black Elk

OUR
RIGHT BRAIN
POTENTIAL

It's almost midnight, the time when some mystery writers believe their best work is done. But as we peer through the drapes and into the cluttered den of a writer I have in mind, he is not writing. For some reason he is making strange sounds and staring at a blank sheet of paper.

The following morning we visit the bedroom study of a well-read children's book author. It is a little past nine and her youngsters are in school. Her husband has been at his office since eight. She has six delicious hours for her work. But she is not writing either. Instead, she is smoking and pacing and muttering. Why?

There is a very good chance that if it were possible to monitor writers in this country and abroad, we would find many of them grappling with the same invisible presence: a two-headed monster whose insatiable appetite consumes creative energy with one head as the other devours our confidence. The beast is commonly known as *writer's block*, although there are a number of unprintables by which it is called.

Writer's block is more than the inability to write, it's a writing sickness. One example is the novelist dashing off a fifty-page segment of an eagerly awaited book—but for some reason the pages read like the directions on a soap box. Then there's the beginner with a great idea for a first book. But the idea hangs in midair, refusing to come off on paper. And let us not overlook the published writer whose last book was a best-seller. The world now waits to buy his next one, for which the author has received a large advance. Lucky fellow? Not at all. His first draft was so bad the publisher sent it back with a note stating there must be some error; perhaps the writer sent his son's homework by mistake. Prior to this our writer had been considered one of the new luminaries, with a promising career ahead. Now he is filling out an application for the French Foreign Legion.

Each is an example of the deadly effect of writer's block, on anyone from beginner to best-selling author.

In its simplest form, the block can be defined as an inability to brain-shift from left to right. The brain has two major hemispheres. The left brain deals with routine, explicit functions and directions. The right side generates creativity. The left side is the dominant side, and therefore the shift from left to right can be troublesome.

In simple terms, the left brain does not like to relinquish its authority. This is why artists and writers alike have a painful time asserting their creativity. Of course there are some who never have trouble—they are blessed with the ability to shift into their creativity at will; but such is not the case for the majority. Most of us learn quite early, as we reach for our creativity, that when it is time to shift we endure the twelve labors of Hercules.

Writers find that some of the most difficult times for the shift will be when they have little excitement or eagerness for their project. There is nothing like enthusiasm to lubricate the machinery of our creative function. Money? Yes, money has been known to help, because it is the stuff of our dreams, and dreams are neighborly to our right brain.

This is why writers should make their early projects the ones they have the most personal interest in or excitement for. This makes writing different from childhood, when we were forced to eat our vegetables first and then get our dessert. Writers are allowed to have their dessert first. Then, after building confidence, they branch out into other territories and try out the vegetables of writing. This especially means that the story Uncle Frank said "you oughta write" very likely is the worst topic of all unless you have fervent interest in it.

Subjects that arouse you also arouse the right brain, and you need right brain function to write. Right brain means the difference between typing and writing. Sure, that stack of copy looks nice, but that doesn't mean it is interesting or usable. Writer's block may have infested those pages, and though they are neatly typed they might be dull. Writer's block is sneaky. It's like termites in our creativity.

Writing and typing are quite different. Writing comes from the innovative, visually inspired resources of the right brain. Typing, stenography, is a precise science and not at all creative. Rendering some stuffy bureaucrat's bad dictation is challenging, but most typists are too wise to be creative with their employer's words.

Which brings us back to the original statement, that in order to write effectively the writer must groove in the right hemisphere where originality and innovation are conceived. This is not to state that all the material on the shelves is either new or innovative. Many writers have established a name and thus can write the same stories over and over while getting paid for it. Change the names, shift a setting or two, and away they go. It's marvelous for the writer; he or she sings all the way to the bank.

Others, those who have not reached this vaunted place, must break in with new, exciting stories and styles. Our more fortunate colleagues are not about to share their fiefdoms. Thus, cleverly developed characters must perform in our exciting stories as we work quite hard not to sound like Hemingway or James. This means the new writer must understand and have a firm grasp of right brain perception and its function. Most of all, this knowledge renders us less susceptive to writer's block.

Although it might not help to know this, writer's block is not peculiar to writers. It might very well have been called "sculptor's block," or "painter's block," or even "designer's block." A counterpart in sports might have been named, "Hitter's block," as slumping baseball sluggers hear their coaches tell them, "Hang in there, big guy. It's only in your head." The poor chap knows this. What he doesn't know is what to do about it.

He thinks about little else—and *thinking* is the key to the problem. Fretting about something calls the left brain to the rescue. The left brain is programmed to deal with trouble. It can't change writer's block, but it can shift the mode of concentration. This makes it worse, whether writing or hitting baseballs or carving marble. Fretting is worrying, which is thinking, which in turn locks the left brain into deeper control position. But the left brain can do little about a right brain dilemma—but think about it.

Studies show that stress creates a shift to the left brain, taking away the right's dominion. Lessening stress is very important to enhancing creative concentration. One thing that helps is to establish a time of stress-free occupation prior to writing. For the writers with easy access to their right brain, this is not a concern. For others, it will take time and patience and practice. In general, our creativity appears more frequently when there is less stress and more of an element of welcome. The expression of amusement or fun is more conducive to right brain shifting. These are times when the left brain is not alert, times when a sudden creative flash is more likely. A time of emotional or mental lull is ideal for creative occurrence.

For example, you are trimming the lawn and an unexpected inspiration appears. It has not come at the most convenient time, but creativity can be described as a maverick factor that is capricious and rarely subordinate to command. It comes to the humble as well as to the mighty. Some farm lad might devise a way to make gasoline from well water. George Washington Carver, a slave-born Black, figured out how to turn peanut shells into paint by using a knowledge of chemistry and his very creative mind.

The incidence of inspiration seems to stem from those moments when the mind is suspended from surrounding distractions. Athletes say this is what allows them to function as though they were in slow motion. "When I was hitting the ball well," home-run king Hank Aaron once said, "the ball seemed to come over the plate so slowly that I could read the trademark."

Equally important is knowing that the left brain is no villain. It has a job and does it very well. The left brain evolved into its position of dominance as the species moved from the caves into technology. The left brain helps us remain between the yellow lines of the freeway, figure our income taxes, make logical decisions, and apply a vast library of lessons learned through trial and error. It is linear, factual, and tends to our well-being. If the house is on fire, the left brain calls the fire department and runs for the water hose. The right brain admires the fluorescent tones of red in the blaze.

Right brain is the innovator. It resists rules and regulations that inhibit its creative development. It is holistic, daring, and visionary. Risks, adventure, the unknown, all fascinate the right brain. Here is the cutting edge of advancement as surely as yesterday's fantasy is tomorrow's reality.

Generals Eisenhower and Patton were fine examples of right and left brain expression. Ike was master of detail and order: Patton was the unpredictable genius of tactical exploitation. Ike was an analyst, a linear thinker. Patton was fanciful, a believer in reincarnation who relied on intuition to a shocking extent. Ike lived by the book. Patton broke the rules.

The left brain has not always been dominant. In our more primitive state, when we relied on signs, spirit guides, and dwelled in superstition, the right brain was dominant. Today we rely on technology, which is the precise use of exact formulas. For this reason our schools too are heavily affected by technology (left brain). And our customs and social conditioning all are related to logical, orderly systems. Anyone who doubts this should put ice cream on their mashed potatoes the next time they attend a formal dinner. The reaction of the guests, all conditioned to the precise rules for dinner behavior, will be evidence enough.

Yet, is this all bad? No, it is necessary in view of our overpopulated conditions. We need regulations and rules, even for meals. If the present world was one of right brain dominion we would have disorder beyond anything imaginable. All our laws would be creative, adventurous, innovative, spontaneous, and artistic—but hardly practical. Imagine 200 million Americans artistically running red lights, jaywalking, not paying taxes or worrying very much about it all. Visions, fantasies, and dream messages would be the rule of government. In fact, there are detractors today who will suggest that the aforementioned conditions already are in force in government.

But the interest here is in writing, not government. Our point and goal is to gain balance in right and left brain status, with easier access to our creativity.

Our existing society is not an equal opportunity condition for right brain expression. The left has become so dominant that it becomes increasingly difficult for it to relinquish control to the right side. In earlier times, for instance, women had time to quilt, design clothing, and tend flower gardens. These, at least, were glimpses of creative opportunity. But today it is cheaper and more practical to buy a quilt or a jacket. A bunch of flowers? Call a florist.

"This is why I was so thankful for our adult education classes," a woman from the first group said. "This course has been a survival kit for me." Her profession as a computer programmer offered little chance for creative expression. And in class she had the chance to exercise her right brain and share the results with others of similar desire. Best of all, the group was supportive and there were few if any negative factors.

A magazine article on right brain perception likened linear versus creative thinking to a pair of brothers, one of them logical, orderly, and specific, a fiend for details and deeply committed to the rules and regulations. The other would be imaginative, entertaining, and full of new ideas.

In order to express those new ideas, the creative brother needed the keys to the control room. But the orderly brother was in charge of those keys and when asked for them, refused.

"No way," he declared. "No visionary, bohemian dreamer is going to ruin my orderly facilities—not even my own brother." The creative brother could see at this point that it was going to take some manipulation to use the control room.

The orderly brother could see the whole system going down

the pipe if his creative counterpart got the keys. Assuming that the dominant brother is convinced it's all right to let the other have the keys for just a few moments, it is highly likely that Lefty watched from the shadows with great anxiety. This anxiety is how the mind works even though the right brain is in control. The left hovers about, worrying loudly to such an extent that the creative experience is shallow at best.

Yes, the left brain does have a technical appreciation of the right brain's advisory and backup capability. But in other than an emergency, the left side prefers to dominate, and it fills this role to such an extent that our life functions are sadly deprived of creativity. Yet in some of us, the right brain has such power, due to greater access, that the left is more regularly suppressed. This was most apparent in such visionaries as Ben Franklin, Thomas Edison, and George Patton.

In putting these patterns in place, we find a vicious circle. The interruptions, anxiety, and disturbances that are part of our lives keep the left brain with one finger constantly on the red telephone. Creativity has little opportunity unless the individual decides to learn how to share right and left brain expression. Unfortunately, our left brain has learned to appeal to our inherent laziness; it coaxes us away from right brain expression with cheap entertainment, cassette music, and video games. These involvements are the fruit of someone else's creativity—a poor substitute, but they allow the left brain to remain in control.

A helpful direction for shared expression is to establish an ideal environment for creative activity. For ages writers and artists have instinctively sought quiet, less turbulent places for their expression. This was long before we knew about right and left brain differences. It was an instinctive move and is still advantageous.

How fine it would be if we could have such luxury as a place of quiet and little distraction. But as writers, we also are consumers and have to earn money until our writing catches on. To this need, this book is offered. It proposes a way to use both sides of the brain and end a half-witted existence. The principles of right brain expression can be the next best thing to an island hideaway. One can work in the very eye of a hurricane because it's possible to turn off the mind (left side) with practice and persistence. After all, news writers have been doing it for years.

Writers must produce in fair weather and foul. Mother writers have to stop and make peanut butter and jelly sandwiches that leave grape stains on their pages. Father writers must stop their work and fix things, which leaves bike lube on their novels. This is the way life is.

The first step to take is to plan your writing time at the least disruptive time of day—or night. A woman once completed a novel writing between midnight and 3 A.M., when her family was sleeping. When it was published they were incredulous—they didn't even know she was writing. But a few hours at that time of day are worth six with disruptions. Peace and quiet, though, are not the total answer. Our children's book writer a few pages back was working with her children in school and her husband at the office. Her environment should have been ideal, and it was—she just needed help with the next step: shifting left to right.

Shifting to right brain demands that we first realize that obstructions lie betwixt the two. Many of them are from child-hood, the early *don'ts*. Remember them? *Don't* spill, *don't* draw on the wall—ad infinitum.

These don'ts are programmed into the brain's alert system and become rules of real importance. It is not uncommon to find adults still fanatically cleaning up their plates. If you don't, the Hottentots will starve. Remember? Knowing this is in your brain helps you deal with it. One of the famous writers in a later chapter tells about not being able to begin writing on a clean piece of paper. He uses an old envelope to scribble his early ideas, and not until he feels his ideas have merit does he dare put them on white paper. Can't you imagine his early don'ts?

Now you might see how the evil demon, writer's block, can use this. I suspect that the left brain is in league with this beast to retain dominion, although this is not conclusive. Still, the don'ts are a means of leverage, and they do represent rules. And the left brain does its job—sometimes too well.

Let us take this idea a bit further. Consider the indoctrination of early life. Think about how proud parents are when their baby arrives, how elated they are when it first walks and talks. Pictures are taken and relatives phoned long distance. The mailman, grocer, and any neighbors careless enough to be caught outside locked doors are strong-armed into watching our toddler perform, hearing it say "Mama."

Not long after that little one is walking and talking, things change. Now it is warned to shut up and sit down. Little wonder our command of creativity can be timorous. We know it's in there somewhere, but we don't want to break any rules.

By comparison, let us investigate the so-called primitive cultures, more right-brained than left. They live with visions, intuition, dreams, and spirit guides. They envision life in every object, living and inanimate. The American Plains Indians saw everything as part of the overall spiritual family in which we are all related as brothers and sisters. Locusts, earthworms, antelope, buffalo, rocks, streams, trees—each had a dignity in the Indian sense of worship. Each entity was known to have a spirit and was given great respect and regularly asked for advice. For these considerations thanks were given and prayers and offerings made. This is right brain.

The Indians were well attuned to their dreams and visions, placing great reliance in them. The tribal leaders and holy men fasted and steam bathed in sweat lodges, seeking guidance and advice from the spirits for war parties and hunting bands. We know today that fasting and steaming bring on a hallucinatory state from which visions are possible. The credibility of visions is growing, and crime investigators are beginning to ask clairvoyants for help in solving murders.

Today a variation of the steam bath is being used to enhance the higher state (right brain) of the mind's perception. One is the use of tanks filled with body-temperature saline solution where you float in womblike security. Exquisite creative concentration has been possible in these tanks, and the emotional serenity achieved is said to be amazing. After all, frustration is known to be a severe ingredient in stress, and the tank experiences might provide proof enough of our need to insulate our creative powers.

Some writers feel that tanks for stress studies would not be needed if there were more provision for creative expression in the schools and college systems, if the creative departments had the same status as the sciences, for example. The educators cry out, "We do provide for creative outlets." But this is done on left brain terms—the left brain system runs the facility, the department, and education as we know it. And using left brain terms for right brain expression is like giving sawdust to a thirsty horse.

The success or failure of an educational concept pivots on funding, and funding, for example, for "Basic Sweat Lodge," or "Visions Through Fasting—Intermediate and Advanced," has little chance. Not to mention "Creative Saline Tank Immersion."

The total human function does not do well on a sustained diet of predictable logic. There are times when we scream for something original, exciting, fresh, or innovative. Left brain existence can become so overwhelmingly boring that it might explain the excesses of alcoholism and drug abuse. When questioned once about marijuana, an abuser said, "I'll tell you one thing, man. It ain't dull." Of course it is not dull. In fact, it's a destructive means for establishing right brain. So starved are the minds of millions for something creative that Detroit changing auto models every year and Dior lifting or lowering the hemline have become big events in our lives.

Creative people seem instinctively to realize this and hold tightly to their own creativity. At times they seem to be working overtime at being exciting or different. Through eccentricity, the left brain is tuned out and the right established. Here might be an example of self-hypnosis, a way to psych out the left brain for a longer grasp of the right.

Tom O'Brien, a southern California journalist and writer, once said, "It's no fun being Irish if you can't make a fool of yourself once in a while." Which does apply to writers: the outrageous novelist marrying his ninth wife, the sculptor streaking yet another party, a silly screenwriter typing the last scene of a sea adventure—underwater. All are examples of the creative mind grasping for anything that will perpetuate its creativity.

To overcome the problems of writer's block, it helps to understand the side of the brain from which writing comes. Here is an example of the right brain's thinking: You have the simple problem of two and two making four. But the right brain sees the creative potential. It is more innovative and pleasing to the eye when $2 \times 2 = 22$. The rows of 2's are more symmetrical, a fine design for wallpaper margins. Or a closer examination might show that the twos actually are ducks, with the addition of a bill and tail.

$$\text{🦆} \times \text{🦆} = \text{🦆🦆}$$

It's enough to give your arithmetic teacher dyspepsia, but you must admit they are cuter than anything else that comes to mind. And they are right brain.

Most left brain thinkers find this rather trite. But that same logical person is the one we see in the papers who has taken off on a hang glider tour around the world or has decided to break the world record for rowing a boat up the Mississippi River. Left brain dominates are just as starved for full expression of their brain as creative people. A right brain famine is closing about us and no one is spared. Writing is a good way to escape.

As a species we have come a millenium from times when we were right brain dominant and the left had little to do but remember how to prevent a lion from eating us. Today we must honor the rules of the road, file taxes, and participate in a highly complicated social system whose rules and regulations fill our mailboxes, blast us from radios and television, newspapers and magazines. In turn we preach these same messages to our children, causing their creativity to drift farther into the sea of little use.

That child we read about a few pages back, the one who was learning to shut up and sit down, also is learning how to lace up shoes, get the proper shoe on the proper foot, and eat spinach. By age eight the child is well on the way to becoming a part of the left brain generations lockstepping their way into the future. The way ahead is marked with don'ts: Don't spill, fall, cry, wet the bed, mark the walls, fight, argue, talk back, talk with your mouth full, make a mess, pull the cat's tail, or eat the dog's food.

Despite what we think we know about the brain, our knowledge resembles an adventurer's tent in the midst of the Russian Steppes. We know the brain is divided into hemispheres, right and left; that it is connected by a narrow pillar of nerve material, the corpus callosum. We know our functions continue when the corpus callosum is severed; and we know that when damage occurs in one hemisphere, the other is capable of taking over many of the damaged partner's functions. But we do not know how it all works, nor can we explain why the more gifted persons are not necessarily the most successful. Is there some penalty for being gifted? Why are the most talented people so often the least productive?

It would be helpful to know why some writers can lay their work aside for lengthy periods and then return to their old form with no trouble. Others of us have a devil of a time relocating that keen groove we held.

We do know from experience that writers who write regularly, with no long periods of layoff, retain that groove. Ray Bradbury, the prodigious science fiction writer, swears by this rule. "Write something every day," he urges.

Max Brand, a western writer of legendary production, also believed in writing daily, no matter what. It was said that once, with his family on a European vacation, Brand enjoyed the old-world sights while making notes for his next western novel. His shoot-outs, cattle stampedes, and barroom brawls were done thousands of miles away from their dusty prairie settings.

Keep in touch with your writing groove. Max Brand and Ray Bradbury always stayed close to theirs.

An astute college professor, Betty Edwards is a widely acknowledged student of right and left brain perception. Most important of all, she compiled a publication that brought the principles of right brain comprehension to classroom level. Her book, *Drawing on the Right Side of the Brain*, (Tarcher Publishing, 1979) provided a significant, clearly explained explanation of right brain perception that is ideal for student use. Most writers are amused when they find that the book was written for drawing, not writing. But the principles are the same, and no finer work for basic study of right brain principles is to be found.

The late Robert Kirsch, Los Angeles *Times's* book reviewer, said in 1979, ". . . the book is emancipation." *Drawing* showed how the native creativity of a child is effectively blunted before second or third grade. In other words, our access is limited even before we have full grasp of it. Writer's block is one of several symptoms of that limited access.

No gathering of writers is possible without someone talking about that "something" that slows progress, that wasteland of white paper staring back without compassion.

Some of the complaints are so impressive they should be submitted for publication. Upon hearing, "Writing is like the dry birthing of a horned demon; a caesarean without anesthetic," no wonder so many new writers decided to be accountants or plumbers. Dry birthing? What malarkey. Writing can and must be rewarding, for reasons other than publication. Writing should be fun; the exhilaration of right brain expression make it so.

A good example is the writer who has finished a good day's work and can't wait until the next day to edit. There is a certain excitement here that has nothing to do with money or fame. It has to do with enjoying the work at hand. Reading the work of the day before is like opening a present; each sentence holds some surprise. There's a reason for this: We read with the left side but write with the right.

In learning how the brain relates to writing it is also important to explode some of the writing myths that exist. One of the most common is that you must have a strong background in English and grammar. Writing has nothing to do with either. English and grammar are editing skills, and writing is not editing. Were English the fount source of writing success, there would be a lemminglike stampede to the nearest junior college. Of course, college is bound with rules and regimentation, which are anathema to creativity and right brain ascension. The creative mind, bound with rules and regulations, finds itself heading south to catch a northbound train. Many potentially fine writers have been discouraged by this, and those who succeed do so in spite of it. A degree is not carte blanche to instant publication or critical success as a writer. There is strong evidence that too many English graduates are writing and too many writers are driving trucks.

Colleges and universities cannot help but become cloning depots for left brain thinking. They are captives of their own structure. Hemingway is said to have advised young writers to get into life and experience it rather than spend time in pursuit of nifty titles and degrees. In his experience, Hemingway added, he drew on his life and past relationships—not his education. Get into life, young writers are urged. Get seduced, lost, drive a cab, drive a truck, meet people and listen to them. In this way you establish a store of life experiences to draw upon. Each of us has an observer inside. The more we see and experience, the more effective and real our creative renditions will be.

And this is not to state that college is a waste of time. Not everyone in college is there to become a writer, and a lot of writers survive the system rather than benefit from it. Just remember that the years spent in college will be full and rich if approached with awareness. But let there be no mistaking that the left brain is not king. It *is* king, and there is little tolerance for right brain exceptions. As a result, bright-eyed grads come forth every nine months or so like peach pits from a cannery. They have studied the same books and heard the same lectures their instructors heard when they were in school. The quotes they have memorized are quotes from the same literary giants their instructors once memorized.

Now the grads are seeking jobs. Woolf, Joyce, Hawthorne—all were fine and viable in school, but interviewers are looking for people with new ideas, people with right brain potential. Sadly, our grads have been prepared in left brain institutions. Their right brain proficiency has not had equal training. But if our young graduates are lucky, they might be hired to edit some cabdriver's ungrammatical but stunningly original novel. Degree and all, our grad has become a mechanic for other people's creativity.

In class we are asked, What is creativity? Where is it? How can I find it? And I am reminded of the late Euell Gibbons, a naturalist and author of *Stalking the Wild Places*, which tells how an individual, faced with survival, actually starved while in the midst of edibles. Roots, buds, leaves—all might have sustained the victim, but he had no knowledge of where or what there was to eat.

In writing it is much the same. A bounty of material surrounds the writer. All that is needed is access to the creative mind, a mind that can take a crumpled paper and build a story about it: where the paper came from, how it was found, the drudgery and drama of the calloused hands that made the paper possible. Also, the right brain can be stimulated with creative games and exercises—writing exercises that stimulate imagination.

The human capacity for creativity has barely been scratched for potential. Only recently has it been realized that intelligence quotient (IQ) is no more important than creative quotient (CQ). Therefore the true measure of brain capacity has not been used, and without question, a lot of children have suffered. Genius, for instance, has been mistaken for retardation. Right brain versus left brain.

It takes little imagination to realize that the right brain reflects the future, while the left brain deals with the *now* of information. The left brain represents the box of all known information. The right brain represents the information we are yet to accumulate. The fantasies of the old comic book hero Buck Rogers are no longer make-believe. They are now happening. We are in outer space. We are using space belts and rocket ships and space stations.

Five hundred years ago Leonardo da Vinci, the fifteenth century wizard, designed wings so that people could fly. At the time he was considered eccentric. Now, he would be on the *Today Show* and the six o'clock news. We are ready for wings. In da Vinci's time, flight was thought of as the work of the devil.

During times of crisis we see the right brain becoming more dominant. During World War II, when the Allies were so desperately behind the Axis powers in war technology, the right brain was the one resource that closed the gap. Prisoners taken at the first of the war and then released at armistice didn't even recognize their fellow countrymen, so great were the advances in weapons, technology, and even uniforms.

Without some crisis to release the rigidly established left brain institutions, right brain potential is denied. Even as you read this page there is factory worker, a field hand, a young mind of tremendous potential that will never be discovered. We do not recruit creative talent as some nations do, and the most priceless resource of all—right brain power—is not realized. In America we expect the person of great creative potential to bootstrap his or her way to prominence first—then they find recognition.

An interesting example of right brain development is found in the Indian child of 150 years ago. Compare this child with the modern youngster learning to shut up and sit down. The conditioning of the modern child is left brain conditioning. The Indian child was just the opposite. Allowed to roam free, half naked summer and winter, the youngster had a marvelous freedom of expression. There was encouragement to develop a sense of identity and personal expression. Potty training? The child merely went into the weeds when the urge so moved him. There was a whole prairie on which to run and whoop. The child had a sense of independent expression our modern youngster will never know.

In maturity, the Indian lived in harmony with the environment. Suicide was rare, as were most modern neuroses. The Indians lived with visions and prayed to their gods, made medicine, and prospered. Many of us would gladly exchange our washer-dryer existence for the spirituality and more equal expression of both brain hemispheres.

So right brain were the Plains tribes that they placed a higher value on touching an enemy during an encounter than on slaying that enemy. Sadly, the more logical, linear-thinking whites believed that a good enemy, Indian or otherwise, was a dead enemy. But for one remarkably romantic period in history, the example of the Plains people became testimony to right brain perception and expression, a people's grasp of spiritual, creative, shared brain existence.

The relationship of all this to writing will distill into your ability to write on the terms of the twentieth century or not. We cannot return to the days of the American plains. Each day it becomes harder to lose sight of a building or an auto. But we do have a place to go, the place of our writing resources. The right brain will lead us there, and it will be helpful to accept that all of a sudden it is okay to daydream, fantasize, and wool-gather. Such is the stuff of creation. In the process, you will begin to find touch with a deeper sense of satisfaction than ever before.

MAKING
THE SHIFT

When you describe crossing over to right brain," a member of our creative writing group said, "you make it sound like going to heaven." The rest of the class was amused by her observation. But she was right on.

"When you've been blocked as long as some of us," she was reminded, "it is not *like* heaven, it *is* heaven."

The poet of our group said that for him, "it's like leaving the shadows of frustration to bask in the warm sunshine of my creativity. The words flow evenly and agreeably. I am totally secured in my writing groove."

The M.D.-mystery writer said, "When I glance at the clock and see I have been writing for several hours, I am stunned. I seem to lose all sense of time. Once my wife said she phoned me to see if I was home and though the telephone was at my side, I did not hear it ring."

All of the above are right brain identifiers: the lapse of time awareness, near oblivion to all but the most strident interruptions, a strong sense of participating in the scenes being written, and deep satisfaction when the writing ends.

Writers' spouses who complain about their mates being so involved their writing might go on as the roof was lifted from over their heads are right, almost. Maybe if someone came into the writer's study to move the typing stand to make room for the bulldozer, then the writer might look up from the western shoot-out chapter, the torrid love scene, the critical moment of the mystery. But don't count on it. I remember an article on the western writer Louis L'Amour in which he did a few pages of his novel in progress with the typewriter and stand on the double yellow line on Wilshire Boulevard in Los Angeles. It was noon; it is said that pedestrians are skittish about crossing Wilshire and say their prayers even when the green arrow is in their favor.

Such an extent of right brain concentration is possible because writers of the ilk of L'Amour have paid their dues by pounding smooth the avenues to their right brain perceptions. The L'Amours probably have little knowledge of or interest in shifting left to right; they shift on command and that's enough.

For newer writers, there now is enough known to provide a few guidelines for shifting into creativity. No longer must you work years and struggle endlessly while establishing a right brain system. The first thing to accept is that there are some who have easier access to their creativity than others. The easy ones we'll call "Easy Shifters." They seem to have a blessed, automatic connection with their right brain. Generally, they have been voracious readers with a goodly amount of early freedom to indulge their fantasies. This category of writer has a lot in common with the super athlete, the kind who makes impossible feats seem easy. An example is Julius Erving, the loop-armed genius of the Philadelphia 76ers basketball team. He makes leaping lay-ups fifteen feet from the basket, then is puzzled when observers rave.

Or what about the gifted senator from Illinois, the late Everett Dirksen? He was another natural who could deliver a two-hour speech without notes or previous preparation, then shrug it off as though it were something everyone did.

Easy Shifters have access to the mechanism that turns off all outside activity or distraction, enabling them to focus on what they have to do. They function in busy boulevards; in hectic, smoke-filled offices; or frantic basketball courts.

Moderate Shifters have equal right brain powers, but have more trouble in stating them. They work and persevere and learn to live with their slower access, though their work can be as effective as the Easy Shifter. There are techniques to help the Moderates, but they seem to agree that writing regularly serves them as well as anything. They stay in touch with their writing muscle.

"After a page of work," one of them said, "I drift into right brain and almost see it coming when I do; that opaque curtain as though there were a dim stage in my mind on which the distractions about me have little effect."

The Moderates seemed to agree that "I can routinely throw away my first page or so before I am settled into my groove. But this is how it works for me and I accept it. Sometimes I just write a page of drivel to establish contact."

Difficult Shifters are an advanced condition of Moderates. The Difficults work harder, and in so doing their work seem to be consistently equal to or better than the Easy or Moderate Shifters. They require no greater counseling or stiffer exercises, they merely work harder and often come off with superior work.

The degree of creative blockage for writers can escalate to alarming degrees. Some writers have analysts, so great is their block. But knowing what causes the block can help if by doing nothing more than providing an understanding of it.

In dealing with this block we have learned that the resistance from left brain is a good deal of the problem. Ironically, the left brain has one condition it can not deal with for any length of time: boredom. Writers have unwittingly used boredom for relieving their block without actually knowing what was taking place. But the left brain's control does fade after extensive periods of repetitious, monotonous involvement. A church sermon by some well-intentioned but windy sermonizer can send the mind into distant vistas, seeking escape. Fantasies roll in like morning fog.

I remember Frank Miller, the Pulitzer Prize-winning cartoonist for the Des Moines *Register,* who brought his drawing pad to church and spent the duration of the sermon sketching. The setting was restful and serene, and it would not be fair to say the minister put Miller into right brain. But it's always possible. And Miller did win a Pulitzer. Sadly, writers cannot take their typewriters to service.

The right brain does provide us with sanctuary at times of inescapable circumstance. Solitary confinement is a good example. Having been in solitary confinement in the military, I can personally say it was the most restful, refreshing time of my hitch. Serving time in a bare cubicle is not difficult. You are rarely there. The right brain can take you out of tedious situations; without this the burden might be such that the only alternative would be suicide.

In order to write we need this relief from literal reality, and this means the left brain must relinquish control. When in left brain there is no escape. Prison is prison. The bars on the windows are exactly that. But there is escape, the right brain cries out, and the moment it takes control we are led past the confinement and into our favorite fantasy.

With practice, boredom can be implemented to establish right brain. Another technique similar to boredom is to back into right brain. For instance, initiate some routine task and persist until right brain occurs. A writer once told of having trouble getting started; she decided that it would be wiser to perform some task around the house than to sit around staring at the typewriter. And there was that wall behind the kitchen stove. The grease was very thick and tough to remove. So, the next morning, if writing did not come, she would clean that wall.

"I sat there the next morning and my writing would not appear, so I got up to go clean that wall," the writer said. "Almost instantaneously, the vision I needed appeared. I saw the chapter unfolding as though someone had done it for me. Now that the story is done I give full credit to that wall."

In my own experience, I remember my first day in Physics One. The professor extolled the virtues of small levers to long levers, fulcrums to the divisor of the two. All of this made sense to physics teachers but was Greek to me and of less interest. I sat there not daring to look out the window, where the river wound sensuously along its way. Even thinking about it made my mind leave to wander the riverbank, my body still in class, my mind shamelessly truant. During that time I met a friendly river elf sitting on a mushroom. We had a nice visit before he had to go home to supper. When I returned to class I found everyone gone but me. And on the blackboard there was a message:

> *We decided not to disturb you. There will be no further point in returning to this class since you have failed beyond redemption. Respectfully . . .*

I was not at all discouraged. In a way it was emancipation. Physics One and I were not well mated; I compare it to spring, when mother said we could change from long flannels to BVDs. But I do recommend Physics One to writers who need to shift into right brain.

The shift is like that time when an airline captain, having lifted the ship off the ground and with it locked onto the navigational beam, turns the controls over to the copilot. Unless there is a need to announce the Grand Canyon or some equally important geographical phenomenon, the captain takes a nap.

Our brain pilot functions in much the same way. But should an emergency occur in either the brain or the plane, the captain quickly takes command. The years of education and experience using left brain solutions to resolve problems allow airline pilots—and left brain—to do them well. Their task is not a creative one.

Having dealt with some of the ways to shift into creativity, an additional step awaits. This one was devised for those who have trouble shifting; it provides a way to phase down somewhat before changing modes. It amounts to nothing more than writing a few warm-up lines before confronting the shift. And for those who agonize, this will help them. Others will argue that it is too simple, but the challenge of writing is its simplicity.

Rather than plunking oneself down to hammer away at the typewriter, take a moment to contemplate before starting. This is a lot like the musician warming up an instrument before the first curtain. The writer, too, should warm up his instrument—the brain—before he begins. In this way the shift is easier. Try this: Envision a red dot before your eyes, then close them, holding the dot in place. Create every star in the galaxy as a backdrop.

As you watch, the red dot will slowly move into the maze of stars and planets. Watch it and keep it in sight until finally the red dot is gone. Now, as you open your eyes, a level of greater right brain concentration will await, with the left brain less intense. Begin writing.

There are a number of ways to prepare the mind for writing. Joan Didion, the stunning novelist-observer, tells about driving the freeways as a way of gathering her thoughts and preparing for her writing—but not at the tangled times of bumper-to-bumper traffic. She chooses those hours when there is room to cruise.

Some writers will jog and others lift weights to prepare their minds. Meditational periods and yoga sessions all are fine ways to prepare. Each is a way of tempering the left brain's control in preparation to shifting right.

An excellent description of right brain is made by the experience most of us have shared—driving in traffic which is pleasantly flowing as our thoughts and attention wanders into the clouds. The sky is patterned with splashes of cumulus fluff. An easy wind moves them into changing forms and the mind drifts with them. As this happens, a troublesome character in a story suddenly becomes clear. We are eager to get home and make notes, but somehow we are two miles past our off ramp. This is right brain.

Another driving experience with right brain occurs when you arrive at your destination and suddenly snap alert. You don't remember driving through an area on your way home. Did you drive through the stoplights on the way? That portion of your journey is missing.

The lulling effect of mile after mile of highway driving is the stuff of right brain shifting; it might explain the creative minds of some cab drivers and many truckers. Writers commonly use driving to aid their creative shift—many do it instinctively. Newspaper reporters have done it for ages.

Another way for preparing to write or shifting into right brain is to use some dull, repetitious article or news story to establish the left brain's vulnerability to boredom. Few pages are as dull as the stock market pages and business index sections that appear in most daily papers. The writer merely needs to type such information as though it were dictation to subdue the left brain:

> *The government's index of leading indicators moved down in February for the tenth month in a row, signifying that the recession will linger into spring, the Commerce Department said Tuesday. However, the index's moderate drop of 0.3% was better than figures showing a December decline of 0.8% and the revised drop of 1.2% for January. The board of trade forecasts no new movement.*

These columns are usually somewhat longer than the sample here and are very useful for right brain shifting; its monotonous drone about percentiles becomes numbing and for most of us, one typing is sufficient to push the right brain button. If there is continued resistance, repeat the exercise as many times as needed to make the left brain beg for mercy. You can tell when it is waning—your mind will begin to wander. Stop now and begin your serious writing.

A few of these sessions will indeed add to your respect for the secretaries of the world. Typing such material as part of a daily routine must take a will of iron. It also indicates why secretaries get into trouble—a typist needs a lot of left brain concentration to do this. In the process, the fantasies and visions must float in endless succession about the outer boundaries of their minds. This might be why some executives run through secretaries faster than they do white shirts.

The world of left brain activity about us is largely one of

tension, competition, stress, and frustration that demands intensive concentration on the rules and circumstances. In order to initiate the shift, the left side must be somehow unwound. Keep this in mind when your writing comes with difficulty. Ask yourself why your left brain is wound up and, confronting this, proceed to release it with exercises or meditation of some sort. The ones provided here work.

The next experience for some writers will be an element of left brain persistence even though your writing has begun. You hear a disturbing voice that doubts your intentions, ability, and any chance for accomplishment. This is the shifted left brain still seeking dominance though control is shifted. Ignore it and the level of your creative intensity will deepen until the voice is stilled. Acknowledge it and the wily left side will slowly erode your right brain control until the left is dominant once again.

There was an interesting example of this during one of the first creative writing classes when one of the group who was working on a novel said he mouthed all the shibboleths of our past sessions, with little help:

> *Perseverence; work your way into it; the shift will come with patience; the more you write the easier it will be. The list is a long one. And, oh yes, stop thinking about it and just write.*

All this writer could think of was the maxim from Poor Richard: The way to hell is paved with good advice. His mind was all over the place:

> *Is the front door shut?*
> *Is this the day of my dental appointment?*
> *Did I call Sarah and remind her that Marvin wants Eleanor to call Jim?*
> *Should I make another cup of coffee?*
> *Or cut the grass?*

"I was going bananas," the writer said. "So I went out to cut the grass."

Mindlessly, he shoved the stupid, noisy machine up and down the lawn. But—suddenly—creativity swept into his being. The novel was incredibly clear; it opened up in his mind with amazing detail. He dashed into his study, strewing grass across the carpeting. Images flowed from his mind even before he rolled in that first sheet of paper. The plot now worked. The characterizations worked. The writer was living it and shared the pain of his characters, wept with them, lived the realness of his creation, marveled at the bite of the dialogue. There were parts that were hilarious and he roared. There were others that were crushingly sad and he wept—typing insanely all the while.

Barely noticed was his son, home from school and standing in the doorway of the study. Three hours had passed that quickly.

"You writing?" the lad asked.

"No, I'm cutting the grass, you twit."

"That how come you left the mower running?"

"Good grief!"

So intense had been the right brain concentration of this writer that he not only worked three hours without realizing it, but the sound of the idling lawn mower had not broken into his involvement. This is an illustration of backing into right brain. The greasy wall example was another, and writers often are found trimming trees, sewing, waxing a car, or performing routine tasks about the house. But ask them what they are doing and invariably they reply: "Writing, of course."

Perhaps at this point we should turn off our lawn mowers and slow our momentum long enough to explain that writers in right brain are not in hog heaven. Everything you put on paper while in right brain will not be ambrosia. Nor is every seed planted destined to become a stalk of corn or every sprout a bearing tomato plant. Whether famous or aspiring, we eventually learn that writers have a certain amount of drivel to get out of their systems. And this is not a bad thing.

The drivel is mixed with what might be called "the good stuff." Like mining for diamonds, tons of earth must be sifted to find a few gemstones. And the new writer might find with some shock that the many pages of production accumulated are not all usable.

"Welcome," experienced writers will exclaim. Such is the way it works. Yet there is compensation. It has been said, if somewhat tongue-in-cheek, that upon reaching fame and prominence, those pages of drivel will be eagerly published.

There is no accounting for the quality and fluctuation in writing in particular and creativity in general. But the message for all concerned is to continue to produce in lean times as well as in those times of abundance. For who can explain those times when the right brain will fairly pulsate with creativity? Concentration in the left during these times is difficult. Some newspapers, for this reason, will not hire journalists with book-writing backgrounds, because they know that during a period of production the writer's contributions to the job will be lean at best. Even janitors with novels in progress have been known to do poor work.

The hills and valleys of creativity are a real part of the writer's life. As sure as the right brain can erupt in plenty, it also can cough and sputter and give up no more than a few drops of performance. "Those days," a colleague said, "are when I am delighted with a couple of commas. I just think back to when it was all golden times and every word was precious. In fact, this is what keeps me going."

Creativity pause, writer's block, inspirational blackout, whatever you might call it, there will be times when it shadows the best of us. No career of any length will be without it in some form. It can be tiresomely persistent and raise hob with our confidence. And worst of all, it causes us to think. And *think* is the danger signal.

When creativity is in progress, you will hear the left side attempting to get you to think. The nasty little doubts will pop up about your mind, the annoying little voice that creates enough stress to taint the quality of your concentration—and makes you *think*. And thus we shift to left brain for answers to the things we are thinking about. The right brain is not concerned with looking backward for answers. It projects. But you can believe that old you-know-who is on the spot with lots of help. And, of course, to take control. How ironic that it so capably answers the questions it created in the first place. The "what-if" questions.

There are two categories of what-if questions. The negative what-ifs come from the left brain and are intended to penetrate our creative concentration and facilitate left brain control.

The creative what-ifs play devil's advocate and help us find answers and, additionally, explore the undeveloped possibilities in our stories. First, let us deal with the treacherous ones.

A good first line of defense against the treacherous what-ifs is to have a strong state of right brain concentration going and thus be able to ignore these interferences. They are most prevalent at the earlier segments of a day's writing; if the writer persists they will have no more meaning than the barking dog up the street. A second line of defense is knowing why we are vulnerable to them and then finding the means to render them ineffective.

As writers, we are sensitive to suffering and misery because we must open our most sensitive areas of reception in order to write effectively. We sort out the sounds, textures, and flavors, harshness, madness, and greed; we write it and are affected by it. In the process, our own sense of security can be disturbed.

"We're like safecrackers who sandpaper their fingertips to feel the tumblers in a lock mechanism fall into place," a mystery writer said. In his research he had learned that sandpapered fingertips were the mark of the professional safe man. The trouble being, he noted, that sensitive fingertips were a liability in day-to-day living.

The tender-fingered safe man would be of little help around the house. Carpentry work or even potting a plant would be very painful with tender fingertips. In a way, we writers are in that same bind. It doesn't take a lot of imagination to put ourselves into the same situations we write about. Imagination is a large part of the craft; it also works against us in real life. And the negative what-ifs in league with left brain have us at their mercy.

Suppose you are working and the what-ifs begin: What if I fail; can't do it; make a fool of myself; my husband reads this; my wife reads it; they laugh? Worse, what if it's good and I succeed?

These damnable insecurities literally clutter our writing channel. They become a pain in the apostrophe. What to do?

There is such a thing as poetic justice. What if we use the left brain to resolve these negative what-ifs? Let us apply logic to their illogic, rationality to their irrationality. In a sense, we strip them of their coverings and expose them for what they are.

First, make a list of six of the most persistent. Next, draw a diagram that shows a head like that of good old Charlie Brown in "Peanuts." The round, happy face is ideal. Next, draw a line from either side of the head downward so it resembles a channel. At the bottom of this channel make the round image of a typewriter, so the channel leads from the head down to the machine. There is nothing in the channel, but we will fix that.

At scattered locations make six small circles, one for each of your what-ifs. Then make a line to the margin at either side of the head; on each line name one of your anxieties. Put some on either side of the head. Now, in the clear light of investigation, the little buggers lie there like crabs in a trap. Yes, they do exist but, no, they are not nearly as troublesome under that ridiculous cartoon head as they were in our own heads.

You might compare this diagram with the furnishings in your living room. Even in the dark you know where everything is located. The couch is here, and over there is the coffee table, and with one hand, though it is dark, you can touch that awful lamp Aunt Hazel gave you for Christmas as you turn the corner to the hall and brush one knuckle against the bookcase.

It helps very much to know where everything is, lights on or off. And that is the way it should be with your what-ifs. In time you will be able to anticipate them: "Okay, it's time to what-if about wasting time." And in doing this, you pull the stinger in these annoying little critters.

One writer puts her what-ifs next to her typewriter. If one shows up she doesn't have on her list she adds it and thus deprives it of effectiveness. Best of all, they amuse her, making it seem silly that they once were so deadly. In time, the original ones become obsolete, so the list might have to be updated. As they fade from importance, remember—you have taken the fun out of their little game.

Yes, writing is a mind game. We deal with a reader's mind and an editor's mind and a publisher's mind. Most important of all, we deal with our own mind and must somewhat understand it to do our best work. No longer should you be concerned about those what-ifs from the past that remind you how lazy, non-productive, and stupid you are. These are merely a few of your early "don'ts" surfacing in what-if coverings. The moment they appear, write them down on your list. It will serve them right.

Knowing is a vital word in writing because it means we are realizing that very little in our work is accidental. We work to achieve the highest degree of effectiveness and, in so doing, edit and rewrite for greatest effect. The only luck in writing is that of having found some outstanding idea. But we have no control over other elements, such as the right publisher just happening to pick our work from a stack of manuscripts.

Knowing means developing an idea to its best potential. Writers have systems for doing this, each a bit different, depending on the writer. A lot of writers work in something less than the most ideal or greatest production, but they have been doing it so long that to change them is all but fatal. And for writers just entering their career, it will be helpful to consider the most productive and least time-consuming system.

By now it is apparent that we create from the right side of the brain, so it is not unreasonable to suggest that this creative process be interrupted as little as possible. Yet there are writers who work that way, cutting into their creative flow to read and polish their work every few lines or so. This means they shift back and forth from left to right brain and are painfully slow producers.

"I just can't bear waiting to see what I've done," one advocate of this system admitted. He knows it slows him down, but can't resist stopping to peek.

A more productive system is to write/type the full work session for whatever the allotted amount of time might be. Now, lay the pages aside for the next day's session. This way the writing will season overnight. Come the next day, edit the seasoned pages of the previous day's work. This achieves two things: First, there has been an allotment of space between the writing and the reading. This adds objectivity. Next, it provides a refresher on story and characters, giving an element of momentum to the writing that will follow.

Quite often the excitement of the previous day's creativity will be dimmed a bit after seasoning. Also, areas for improvement will be more visible—but don't rewrite the pages. It is important to forge ahead. The revisions will come in the editing chapter.

"My first pages are like crude oil," a young writer said of her first-draft work on a novel. "There is good stuff, but there are impurities too."

This is part of the process—realizing that the production from right brain is a raw product to be refined. During this process the writer should seek as little outside advice as possible. This is a time of inner communion, and outside opinion often will interfere with the pure, creative resource from which good writing is born. Outside opinion at this time is a distraction. The energy comes from without and has nothing to do with the inner powers the writer is drawing from. There will be ample time to get outside opinions but the birth of the first draft is not that time.

Seek out and trust your inner feelings and instincts. Your compulsion to get an outside appraisal is something to put on your what-if list along with those other insecurities that plague you.

"There are too many writing experts giving advice who are not writing," a keen observer once said.

There is deep satisfaction in having worked out and completed your own effective piece of work. In doing this you will find that there is great merit in your own instincts.

TRUSTING
YOUR
WRITING

The best definition of fine writing is one that describes it as deceptively simple. After all, the most impressive work is easiest to read and understand and yet is not elementary. There are tones and undercurrents in this good work that bring us back to read it again.

The left brain formula for good writing would be one that worked for everybody, like the fine carburetors that are machined from a single block of aluminum. Were our cranial hemispheres made this way, it would be great. But they are not, and though the left brain formulas you will find work wonderfully well for chocolate chip cookies, writing evades the formula as well as the recipe. Our identities are just different enough that the 250 million Americans in this country would have to have 250 million custom-tailored formulas—or else they couldn't be writers.

Norman Mailer's formula for good writing might come out sauerkraut when applied to someone else. Many university experts claim they teach creativity and writing, but such is not true. Yes, a good instructor can inspire fine writing, but teaching it would demand a means for entering the individual's mind in order that an equation of common denominator be used—or should we say installed?

Writers discovered long ago that the moment you try to "think creativity," it escapes. Like the wild horse of my boyhood fantasies, the moment I captured this magnificent beast it no longer was a wild stallion. It became just another saddler.

Like the iridescent hue of the dolphin fish (mai-mai), the instant it is caught and hauled from the ocean, the blazing blues and gold dim before your eyes. These are untamed colors that only exist in freedom, on their own terms. So it is with creativity. It will not be caged or corraled. Try to do so and it vanishes.

36

Attempt to bottle it and stock the markets and it turns into smoke and is gone.

Creativity must be treated with respect and not taken for granted. It is a gift and might leave if abused. And this is not to state that creativity cannot be inspired, nor the terms for inspiring creativity taught. Good ideas may be inspired by creating ideal conditions for such inspiration. But it doesn't always work. It has been said, "Show me a man who claims to manufacture creativity and new ideas and I'll show you a man who is fishing in a bucket."

So how does one become more receptive to creativity and good ideas? The most helpful term is *trust*. Trust Your Writing is the name of this chapter, and trusting is the only means of making reliable contact with the right brain, which plays a critical part.

A well-known novelist said, "My creativity lives in the thickets of my brain, appearing on its own terms to prickle my dreams and cause me to wonder with exasperation why I can't call it up like my poodle."

I asked this writer how she dealt with it and she said, "I have learned to trust it and in turn it trusts me. There are times when my creativity feels like performing, and those are times when it comes out to sit with me like some old friend. Then there are times when it is not in the mood. I trust my creativity and respect these times, taking what I get."

Trusting, we decided, is the vital connection we have with our creative forces. There is reason to believe that creativity enjoys baiting the left brain forces that give advice, coach, tutor, and provide master plans for the purposes of creation. Perhaps it is entertaining to watch the left brain chase about in vain. There is a story about an aged elephant trainer that follows this line of thought. The trainer had been told it was impossible to train an African elephant, so he got one and tried to train it. No matter what the trainer did, it always failed. The stubborn beast would not get up on the pedestal and beg. It lacked an element of intelligence, the trainer decided, and with one final effort, he decided to make his teaching system as elementary as possible. The trainer began by getting up on the pedestal himself to give the elephant the idea. This done, he gave the elephant the staff, and to the man's amazement the beast put the trainer through the complete routine in flawless fashion.

Creativity is much like that elephant—it delights in teaching the teacher. But most important is that you trust it.

In a way, the very structure of teacher-student posture puts the student in a subordinate position. This in itself is enough to turn off creativity, which functions best when focused where the right brain can generate the necessary energy. The sub-dominance of teacher-student status is symbolic of left brain over right. There too, creativity is not to be found.

Artists, writers, and other creative persons are most effective when drawing on their own sources of energy—not the teacher's. Teachers are prone to encourage the students to lean or rely too much on the teacher's own energy. But the inspired teacher will urge a class to turn inward and listen to the voice of their own inner resources, trust their own feelings, and make their own honest mistakes. In doing this, the student comes to learn about trusting the powers within. Independence and confidence result; far-sighted guidance must get due credit.

In our creative writing classes we learned that trusting our feelings brought a new reality to our work. We also found that there are two writers in each of us. The outer writer (or public writer) deals with external forces and manifests the greater diplomacy. The inner writer (or private writer) makes no pretense of public relations, charm, or diplomacy. It loves to play devil's advocate, probe characterizations, and weed out any lack of authenticity. Together, the two produce the work we do, lending it thoughtful introspection along with public appeal. And let us not become too distant to the outside world. That world also is a part of our identity. We live in it and share it with others whom we expect to buy our books and read our writing.

Here is an example of how the two might work in an assignment to interview a charming but controversial woman of the world. We are having lunch.

"Her words have a saucy mischief that is in keeping with her piquant personality," the outer writer murmurs.

"She's a bitch," the inner writer insists.

Depending on how controversial the writer desires to be in this assignment, the words of both inner and outer writer have something to be considered. Yet, the work of greatest incisive impact usually comes from the inner writer, who gives not one whit about what anyone else thinks. Some authors are dominated by their inner writers. Of course, the circumstances do not always justify such a position.

This is the crossroads writers regularly face. Just how critical and incisive can I really be? No teacher can provide the answers to this. When in doubt, go with your feelings.

Meanwhile, the outside world feels challenged to change and control our inner writer. From training pants to laureate crown (should we be so lucky) there is a persistent and vigorous effort to regulate our inner workings.

A lot of creative people cannot bear up under this pressure. Therefore we see a parade of misplaced persons wherever we look. Poets are driving trucks. Truck drivers are teaching school. Is this some stop frame from an Ingmar Bergman nightmare on film? Beware.

There is a multitude of teachers, professors, experts, specialists, workshop leaders, talent scouts, and advisors, all milling around in well-intentioned eagerness to—help? Are they truly anxious to help or are they driven by instinctual forces alive since the cave days to control others and thus secure their own positions? In their zeal to help/control (they even write books), the most primitive urge is satisfied. What greater power exists than that to which we turn for help?

There is a very good chance that the left brain is not satisfied with mere control of its own cranial capacity; it might very well desire to control all the other cranial capacities it confronts. Like the wild stallion that works to collect more mares than he can possibly service, the left brain's need to control might very well spell its demise.

The reasonable use of control, when confined to our own capacities, is highly desirable. What could be better than having control of one's own freedom and devices? Why else did Gauguin flee to Tahiti to paint his best work? The man came into a stress-free environment and had little interference. And is it really true that Michelangelo suffered during his hours high above the chapel floor as he painted the Sistine Cathedral ceilings from a teetering scaffold? Or was the privacy and immunity from outsiders up there so delicious that he spent more time there than originally intended? No advice givers could drop in, interrupt, phone, or make suggestions, much less ask questions. It takes little imagination to envision some unsolicited expert telling Michelangelo: "Mike, old man, you're going real fine. But I think the eyes of that second cherub are a bit too close together." The artist's outer mind would have said politely, "I'll take that under advisement." His inner mind would have said, "Beat it."

The intrusion is not so bad as the actual brain response in which the mind must shift from right brain to left. The right is nonverbal. So in order to talk, creativity is broken off. This makes Michelangelo want to smash you with a paint pot. This done, it takes the artist some time to renew the former level of right brain. The rickety scaffolds must have provided a marvelous sanctuary where some of the artist's finest work was done.

But I need advice and feedback, some writers argue. In reply they must be warned that most often they ask for advice but they want encouragement. We rarely take criticism in exactly the way it is given. Inevitably, we change it or vary it. A compliment or word of praise, by comparison, is somehow chiseled into our memory. Also, praise and encouragement seem to do more for us than criticism, no matter how gentle.

Criticism, advice, and suggestions from our families or those close to us can be deadly, especially in the earlier parts of a career. Take the example of Jean B., who once told her brother that she wrote poetry. He asked to see some of it and, since they had been close since childhood, she shared a few pages with him. But to her amazement, he read a few lines, then took his pen and began writing on her polished pages—a few little helps. Jean was crushed.

Relatives and close friends are much too close to our vulner-abilities to become critics. What they observe is personal since our feelings for them are personal. Ideally, the critic, if such must be heard, should be someone distant but qualified. No therapist would counsel her husband; no editor should criticize his writer wife (if he's smart).

"You don't love me," my own writer wife once lamented when I changed one of her favorite sentences from an otherwise delightful paragraph. Wisely, I admitted to poor judgment and restored it.

When criticism is given, we rarely accept it and apply it as given. We listen, consider, then use some aspect of the sugges-tion but somehow manage to add a bit of our own feelings to the observation. When criticism is refined with some of our own ideas it becomes more acceptable. This done, it is "my own" changes instead of "theirs."

Even good ideas are best when they are our own ideas. If the inspiration comes from some other source, we modify it, if at all possible. My grandmother was such an example during the years she collected recipes. Invariably, she would change a little here and a pinch or two of seasoning there. Now the recipe was "hers" and much improved, no doubt.

Writers will often use this system, especially when they get a suggestion from their publisher. Sure, they try to cooperate as much as possible, "but what do publishers know?" a colleague once asked. He made the changes the publisher requested, but altered them for his own sense of being in charge.

Secretaries have always understood this ploy. Their bosses

regularly come up with great ideas the secretary gave them weeks before. Perhaps it is human nature to put our "brand" on the things we use, tangibles and otherwise. But the need to do so is firmly related to our need to trust our creativity. By putting our mark on the material we feel easier about trusting it.

This does not mean writing should not be edited. It means we trust the creative process which produces the material. We need the raw material, writing, in order to have something *to* edit.

And again, it is important to emphasize that *you* are inside there with your right brain, your instincts and feelings. The advice givers are only guessing, even when they have read your work. They could not possibly know what inner workings of the mind went into what you completed. When they presume to criticize too harshly it is likely that you might become confused. Interpreting what they read and applying that to what you intended can make a somewhat volatile situation.

Listen to advice, but ultimately trust your own instincts and feelings. Learn to apply what you are trying to say to the feelings you are attempting to capture in writing.

We asked a woman writer who regularly captured her feelings with such clarity that her work seemed to come from her soul, "How do you know there is communication between feelings and statement?" "Because it feels right," she explained. We later figured out that the inner writer will waver when a piece of work is not in tune. Since then, her classmates have worked very hard to coordinate word and feeling.

The creative groove in each of us is similar to the navigational beam airliners use to follow their course. When so grooved, writers almost glow in the dark. The sentences they create are lovely enough to lift from the pages and hug. When this happens we know the writer is happily grooved. The anguish, suspense, disappointment, happiness, and fulfillment all are felt as deeply as though they were actually happening. And in a way they are happening; we are giving our words life.

In writing classes there are exercises to bring the writer's feelings in tune with the work at hand. These exercises have to do with using criticism in other than the way it is offered.

First, list all the advice, criticism, and suggestions that have been given. Write them down and number them. Here are a few that were used in class:

- Your villain is too limpid. Make him meaner.
- The plot moves too slowly.
- More description of the town would be helpful.
- It seems they need more than four horses.
- Why do Paul and Jeff drink vodka and beer chasers?
- Make the ending funnier.
- Make the love scene in chapter one shorter.

The Villain Is Too Limpid. Just for the sake of exploration, let's make the villain even more transparent. At this point someone in the class always objects. To do the opposite is not taking the advice. But that's the intent of the exercise—to realize that advice turned inside out will often work as well as in its original state. By reversing the advice, we get a completely different approach. Best of all, it's ours.

The Plot Moves Too Slowly. To this the inner writer says, Let's make it even slower. If nothing else, this approach proves that too much advice is taken too seriously. Also, in slowing the plot, the writer might find better solutions to issues that had been dealt with too swiftly.

More Description of the Town Would Be Helpful. And by now it's obvious that there will be less. In doing so, the writer might possibly find elements of the town that improve the story by being dramatized and not by merely being told. There's an old writer's adage: Show, not tell.

It Seems They Would Need More Than Four Horses. The inner writer thinks about this, then decides that the story will really work best with only three horses.

Why Do They Drink Vodka with Beer Chasers? After a brief consultation, both the inner and outer writers agree: Who cares?

The purpose of this exercise is to show that advice or criticism indicates a change might be necessary. But the advice offered is not necessarily the right change to make. A change to the contrary can very well be a lot more advantageous. In working to the opposite of advice or criticism, the writer can find new directions—all on his own.

During this exploration a lot of confidence is gained in finding to a greater degree that writing is bits and pieces of information that can be shifted about for greater impact. Developing this dexterity is to the writer's advantage. It also enhances the trust so vital to writing.

Writers get as much out of their work as they put into it. This is especially true with characterizations. When the writer breathes life into the characters in a story, they breathe back. When the writer talks to them as they develop, they begin to talk back as well. Ask any experienced writer about talking to the characters in a story and the reply will be, "Of course," as though to say, "Doesn't everyone?"

An early experience with talking to a character came by writing a biography of an old horseman from the Civil War era. He was born of a white father and black mother, growing up with slave status on his father's farm, a blend of autocrat and the lowest estate of human existence. His name was Tom Bass.

In writing this biography there came a time when the words were little more than one-dimensional declarations of fragmented information. The man was not alive, and although he had been dead for thirty-five years, it was time to sit down and talk with him. This is the stuff of right braining; it was a fascinating experience that went something like this:

What were your earliest memories, Mr. Bass?

Tom: I guess I recall the horses most of all. Seems I was more horse than person, back then. I felt close to them. Horses were property and so was slaves.

Did you hate slavery?

Tom: I didn't think about it much when I was young. I just grew up them first years likin' everything around me. The farm, the creatures, and mostly my mama, grandpa, and grandma. Guess I was nigh onto six or seven before I realized I was a Bass. But it was more like bein' a Bass horse or Bass cattle. Different from bein' Bass family.

Was this difficult for you?

Tom: It was strange in a way. Used to look at my father, tall and nice-appearin' man; sat a horse awful good. Yet, he was more like my sire and yet not exactly a father. I had trouble sortin' all that out.

How did this affect you later in life?

Tom: It turned me more to my mama's side. I got closer to her and Grandpa and Grandma, all the aunties and uncles. They was my true family. That half of my blood became what counted. As I did this I began to think less white and work at being more black. Course, I couldn't change my color, and that made it harder. My father was jest about everything a young boy could admire.

Did he treat you like a son or relative?

Tom: Mr. William, that's what I was taught to call him, was proud of me—in a way. Not many seven-year-old boys could do what I did with horses and livestock. But this was not the pride of father for son, it was more the pride of his breedin' powers. I was evidence of his "get," as the horse folks call it when the stallion throws good qualities to the colts.

This conversation with Tom Bass lasted much longer than is needed to show how the intimacy of his characterization was developed—through right brain projection. After this extended conversation with Tom Bass he became more alive in the story. Later, the greatest reward of all was when a reader asked, "How long had you known Tom Bass before writing the biography?" When the book was published Tom Bass had been dead almost forty years.

A good lesson was gained from the Tom Bass conversation. I rarely fail to talk with any and all characters in a story, whether it's interview, biography, fiction, or nonfiction. A writer can have rousing conversations with kings, vikings, horses, meadows, and mountains, through right brain projection and trust in the writing.

There is no finer tool to use in writing than the broad powers of the right brain. A writer is a fool to neglect this marvelous capability. It is also useful in expanding an idea. A term for this is *extrapolation*, which means to build from a single concept or from an unknown into a full-blown creation.

With a character in mind, add a few of the ingredients you have and then expand on that. Your powers of intuition help enormously. Add what you feel or imagine or anticipate. As the personality builds, the workable elements remain and the rest is discarded.

An example of this is William Styron's *The Confessions of Nat Turner*, written with a few scraps of information and a double dip of imagination. Yet the story came forth with such believability that a controversy followed. What was Styron's intent? the critics demanded. Only the writer could answer that.

If a professional writer is using a little information and bits of detail and a lot of imagination and intuition, there will be elements of truth in what evolves. The writer has knowledge of human nature and a feeling from what information and research is available. And if the character is colored by that writer's personality or politics, it should not be surprising. That is all that writer has to work with. The writer's creativity is the major research. And thirteen years in newspaper work have convinced this writer that pure objectivity is something from a managing editor's dreams.

Projecting into uncharted territory with intuition and imagination is fine for fiction. But, you might ask, what about nonfiction? It is logical to assume that guesswork is dangerous for nonfiction. But to the contrary, it can be very useful.

Bits of information with little to connect them can drive a writer mad. There is only one thing to do: Use the most logical circumstances to fill out the empty places. The result is something to work with, even though it might be flawed in places. A flawed profile is better than nothing at all. Also, a lot of pertinent questions form during this process.

Extrapolation of this kind can lead the stymied writer into very rewarding results, because there are times when questions are more helpful than answers. When you have the questions, you can dig in the proper places for answers. This is very similar to the detective work police do in solving a crime.

In television production they call this *brainstorming*. A director and producer will sit with a writer or two and explore the what-ifs that come to mind. They explore a lot of possibilities: Will Grandma Frickett continue her hang glider lessons? The possibilities are endless.

For all this to work, the writer has to believe in the system. It is not another form of make-believe that you haven't done since you played house as a kid. That was early training for what you are doing now—serious writing. Expanding your right brain powers in this way is what writers do. Their characters are not fantasy folks. They are real. Trust your writing and believe in what you are doing. The rest will take care of itself.

When your right brain is working properly, you will be little more than the typesetter. The professionals say, "Let it happen and run all the way to the bank."

At this point new writers should be warned that the trust you place in your inner forces can and does take strange directions. These are right-brain-related forces, and therefore they are prone to take their own form as they develop. The story you begin with might not be the one with which you end. The character you create might be somewhat different as he or she develops. But this is no cause for alarm.

As the right brain creates from the images of its own source, so do we edit when the writing is done to prune our creative developments in the direction intended. Ironically, the creative directions are often better than the ones we drafted originally, and it is not unusual to find that we are adjusting our plots to accommodate the flow of our creativity. How often writers have been heard to complain about how the chemistry of a cast of characters and story are taking charge of the original idea—and improving it. "It's as though some subversive force is changing my story," a young author said.

Perhaps the brain has a mixing chamber in which the major elements of a story (plot, characters, setting) are blended into a single coalescent strand. Nothing justifies the demand to trust our writing as much as this magnificent blend. It comes of an intricacy we still do not understand, but which is closely related to the "voice of wisdom" we often hear and at times, to our regret, do not listen to. There is a point in writing when the story we are telling begins to come alive. When this point is reached, listen to it. Use and trust it when at all possible. Listen for this voice of writing wisdom. We all have it. Some writers liken it to a spiritual energy.

Here is an example of the creative inner forces taking off on a tangent. It happened with a western novel written years ago. A character in the story left Tennessee with his sixteen-year-old bride, a yoke of oxen, a milk cow, and much courage. Their destination was Texas.

This vignette was intended as a bit of background for one of the major characters in the story. But the man and his bride grew stronger with each page, until they were creating more energy than the original story. The writer began to wander farther afield from the plot as sons were born and the Texas family built a cabin and staked out land for a ranch. In desperation, the writer had to amputate the vignette to save the novel. It was painful but inevitable and only when the vignette was cut could the writer renegotiate the story, getting back on course.

Ironically, the vignette was later sold as a short story. The completed original novel still reposes—unpublished—on the writer's shelf. Nor is there any question about which direction should have been taken.

No writer is immune to this experience. A plot is the result of left brain planning. The adornments of our creative resources are what we attach to this structure. So why do we wander afield?

An insatiable question mark glows within each of us. We never lose the unquenchable desire to wonder, What if? A child has this quality and expresses it when asking Mother: "What if birds barked?" "How come I can't fly when I flap my arms and jump off the roof?" "What if the sun got lost?" For this very reason, our writer's mind sees possibilities that might differ from the plot: Suppose the wagon turned the corner here instead of continuing down the street? Which is contrary to the story, but—what if?

The less experienced writer will be more tempted by this than the seasoned person who has been through it before. The seasoned writer usually has a stronger plot which allows fewer temptations, but that writer does not allow the mind to become insulated to other eventualities. After a bit of experience writers learn that the mind often knows best—and trust it. Most of all, do not allow those tempting digressions to drift away. If they persist, jot them down and put them in your idea file.

News reporters learn to listen to their writer's mind. It is more than a source of hunches. The assessment of facts and possibilities all are filtered and then responded to in much the same fashion as a printout from a computer. No one would dream of tossing away the result of a computer assessment. Yet we regularly shrug off the printouts from the finest piece of equipment ever known, the human brain. "Trust" should be tattooed on our foreheads.

Bob Woodward and Carl Bernstein, the Watergate reporters, are a very good example. At one point most of their information was little more than a bit of high-percentage guessing. But as one possibility after another developed, there was more solid information to work with and less guesswork. In the end they broke a story that prevented American government from taking a dangerous direction.

At a less sensational level, reporters on beat assignments regularly use a little bit of information and a lot of imagination to flesh out their stories. Some writers call this a nose for news. It might be better called a mind for news.

Investigative reporters and writers all share a fear of asking stupid questions. They also worry about blurting out some unrelated question. An official with a crooked nose might have been a boxer. The executive secretary who subconsciously sits with her feet in the first position of ballet might have been a dancer. Writers notice these things though they have nothing to do with what is being written.

"Once," a writer said of meeting a congressional consultant for an after-hours cocktail, "I asked if his nose had been broken when his wife hit him with a niblick after finding a motel key in his coat pocket?"

The consultant laughed and said, "No, she hit me with a bath brush."

The writer was amazed. Such an element of clairvoyance was scary. Had he read it? Heard it from someone else? Or did he really somehow perceive it in a telepathic sense?

Writers must be reminded that at a time such as this the left brain will argue: "Ah, don't be silly. This fellow's a deacon of the church, a past member of the city council. Son of a respected family that donated the stained glass in the Presbyterian Church."

The right brain is not concerned with this. The left is annoyed. It hates to be made to look foolish; to exceed the bounds of proper behavior (remember those early don'ts). The right brain vibrates with what-ifs, the left with an instant reply of all the calamities that can result. But, voila, the right brain's instincts were right on. A fine story resulted, and guess who is right up front to take the credit and slurp up the praise? Mr. Left Brain, of course. Right brain has no interest in applause. Applause is for accomplishments past. There's the janitor at the courthouse who walks with a limp. I wonder . . . ?

Left brain stories are predictable. In a mystery the writer implies a left brain direction but takes a right brain detour. In order for a mystery to work there have to be those moments of left brain logic with stunning right brain confrontations or else the reader becomes bored. But the writer's imagination is what keeps the reader turning pages. If logic were in force that reader would put down the book and get some sleep.

Some writers have developed the fine graphic power of description and right brain intensity that elevates their work above most others. The late Tommy Thompson's *Blood and Money* has an autopsy scene that will lift your hair. It does not merely describe, it takes you there—much too closely, in fact.

Trusting our instincts and right brain powers has been evident throughout history. Christopher Columbus is a good example of one man's resistance to left brain logic as he sailed beyond the perimeters where errant vessels were thought to go over the hemispheric edge. But with his right brain, three ships, and a crew of little courage, Columbus changed the concept of our world. So did Ben Franklin, Madam Curie, Edison, and the American space program.

Investigate more closely the conflict of logic versus daring. As we push into uncharted territories, the left brain whispers, "I don't like this." The right says, "What the heck."

"You must be insane."

"What if we find something?"

"What if we get killed?"

"What if we don't?"

As writers we must be more than daring, we must be observers as well. Like monkeys, we are people watchers. If one were to reply to the question, Are writers different? The answer would be Yes. The difference is that writers are always writing. Everything we see, hear, or wonder about is applied to some inside scale that measures story possibilities.

The roofer is not always roofing, nor is the carpenter always nailing nails. They finish their day and have a cold drink. The writer might have one too, but the writer is never off duty. That inner writer, like a built-in telephone answering machine, is always on. "Beware of what you say," a mystery writer said to me. "You might appear in my next novel."

Realize too that writers often produce wonderfully creative books that don't make much money. After all, our right brain is not concerned with money. Money is left brain; it is logical and makes sense, but it is not creative. As far as right brain is concerned, a million dollars is only a pile of green paper. Diagnose our system: We take a right brain idea, apply a left brain direction, develop it with right brain creativity, and try to sell it for left brain money.

It helps to accept from a creative point of view that we benefit from adversity; if we're poor, unsold, and unappreciated we might be getting ready to do our best work. Perhaps comfort is left brain—since we all *think* we need it so much—but it does not necessarily make a good writer. Under difficult situations we can come up with inspired ideas.

In a case of beginning writers, the most difficult period is that in which they must be brought to confront their bad experiences. "You only want negativity?" they complain. It takes some time to bring them around to accept that adversity can be the most fascinating part of a story, life, or situation. The problem with writing is that we can't transpose our pain without experiencing it.

As a class project, a group of writers was urged to read some pornography for the experience of knowing about what they rejected. The proposal was made from a purely intellectual point of view, and some of them did admit to a certain curiosity about the seamier sides of life.

After that the class discussed those pornographic stories. Most were surprised at the quality of some of the writing. Then the class was challenged to write a few lines of porno, or at least to compile what they thought was pornographic. After writing this they were to destroy their pages but discuss at the next session any discovery that was made.

Some of the class agreed to do so; others wondered if we might have gone too far. But they were good sports. After all, we were pioneering, to an extent. And only one woman said unequivocally that she would not touch this assignment with a forty-foot pole and probably would not come back next week. The group parted on that note.

The following week we reassembled with all present, even our most vocal dissenter. There was a twinkling eye here and a noticeable blush there, and the restlessness of the group indicated that the roll call might be called later.

"I have to confess," one writer volunteered, "I felt so guilty that I tried to explain to my husband. It was three A.M. and he was so surly that I didn't bring it up again. By breakfast he had forgotten or else decided he dreamt it."

Our outraged writer, let her be known as Mrs. Moriarty, was asked if she had reconsidered the assignment.

"I'd rather not discuss it," she snapped with blazing cheeks. For a moment the class was nearly hysterical.

But the point was made. Writers must know about almost

everything. That does not mean we have to write it, but we benefit from knowing as much as possible. The quality of our creative strand is much improved when we do.

There is wisdom in our writing and our inner writer. We must learn to trust them to become effective, and the only deterrent is that strident voice from the left that wonders: "Maybe we should give this some thought."

4

RIGHT
BRAIN
EXERCISE

Easy access to the right brain makes the challenge of writing a lot simpler. Ideas, too, seem to come more frequently. But as certainly as an artist or ballerina spends hours each day working and exploring newer expressions, so must the writer work and challenge the brain and its creative resources.

Several exercises have been devised to further explore access to right brain expression. Some were born in a classroom as theories and later accepted as laudable; others have been shared by colleagues in the same field. One of the most used is one from Betty Edwards's book; it gives an ideal start for writers and artists just establishing awareness of their right brain potential.

Too much of the information on right brain perception has been described as academic, too scholarly, and ponderous. The writer seeking an easier means of expression has no desire to become a brain pathologist—that writer merely wants less of the nagging block that makes it difficult to start and continue. Under closer scrutiny, it becomes apparent that many of the adherents of right brain knowledge are slowly becoming very left brain in their explanation and guidance. And we must add them to the growing list of contradictions that includes:

- Baldheaded barbers who are experts on hair growth.
- Family counselors who are single and have no children.
- Marriage counselors who are divorced.

Perhaps it should not matter. But intellectuality and traditionalism seem to become synonymous and eventually interchangeable. In this process the grasp of right brain perception lessens. The right brain is emotional, sensual, romantic, and analogic. Therefore its definitions are more acceptable by an actual practitioner of a craft; Dr. Edwards is a fine painter, and her own experiences give her words an edge of authority that escapes the pure theorist.

A right brain exercise is, ideally, one of very little rigidity in order to inspire the creativity it is designed to stimulate. There should be some element of amusement or fun or enjoyment in the exercise. Creativity responds to a stimulated state of mind. This in turn enlivens the imagination.

Good teachers with the most success in helping troubled writers have found that moments of levity are essential in dealing with distress. A writer with a difficult block was advised by her teacher that the advice about to be shared came from great genius. The writer smiled and seemed to accept the rapport that developed between them. Their sessions came to be times of growing enjoyment for both. And it was not long before the writer was entrenched in her writing groove.

The following Betty Edwards exercise is one in which the amusement comes of the unexpected development of completion. The exercise is called "Vases and Faces," and it provides a chance to actually *feel* your brain shifting left to right.

You first draw a simple human face (profile) with the nose pointing to the right side of the page. Use about half the paper for this drawing; its expertness is not a factor. If the face has amusing distinctions, so much the better. As you draw this face, name each feature, speaking aloud. Call out "forehead" and "nose" and "lips" as you draw. As you name each feature, it establishes the state of *left* brain used to call from memory the examples you draw upon.

With this done, now draw the same face, this time with the nose facing the left side of the page. This means the nose of your left face will be facing the nose of your right face. *But*—in drawing this same face, you have to match the features and conformation of the left face. To do this, you will have to duplicate the spaces between the two. A feeling of mental conflict occurs; this is the conflict of left brain being unable to cope with the assignment but right brain being most capable in duplicating the spaces. No call is made on the memory for images of forehead or nose. You are using an original concept to complete "Vases and Faces."

So what or where is the "vase?" Merely draw a line across, connecting the top of left's forehead to right's. Then connect the two at the bottom. What formerly was two profiles with their noses nearly touching is an interesting vase of original design.

In reviewing the sensation of right brain, recall that there was no consciousness of time during the drawing. Elements of tension were lowered. The feeling of escape into the right brain was agreeable, and viewing the completed drawing provided an element of amusement. An additional version of this exercise is done by drawing the left profile in as grotesque an expression as possible. Then complete the right side to match. Connect the tops, and the result is something of a baroque vase, suitable for the shelves of a horror film.

Some writers will argue that this exercise is too simple, but such is the result of years in left brain conditioning. Anything worth while, we are taught, has to be difficult or else there is little merit in it. The most laudable accomplishments are those that cause the greatest pain. But the right brain does not exult in pain or staggering difficulty.

Take, for example, the man in southern California who boasts of teaching others to fly kites. He has a handbook of complicated instructions, and the course is very challenging. Those who complete the study get an impressive patch to sew on their shirts to show they have gained proficiency in kite flying—something children once did for fun and moments of amusement.

Another illustration of how we humans make complication out of simplicity is given in the story from India about a swami who found one of his followers had worked nearly twenty years achieving levitation. "I can walk on water," the man said to the swami.

"You have wasted twenty years learning to walk on water,"

the swami said, "when you can cross on the ferry for a few pennies." The wise one merely smiled sadly and continued his journey. Such was the work of a fool.

Writers can learn a lot from this ancient story. We too spend our lives in search of the golden sentence, when in truth the greatest accomplishment of all is mastery of the simple sentence.

Writing clearly comes more easily when we find access to the right side of the brain. One of the games that help to explore this is played with words. A number of them are given and then the writer selects one, from which a few lines are written with no more intent than to find out what happens. The process is interesting because one word can stimulate another.

To begin, writers are asked to sit comfortably, breathe deeply to gain relaxation, lower the shoulders, and limber the hands. A feeling of freedom and growing easiness will come as you await the first word. Allow each word to drift through your mind as would a leaf from some high branch. If that word falls to the earth without some thought or image appearing, listen for the next.

If you are doing this exercise alone, use a piece of paper to cover all but the word you are dealing with. Should there be some verbal impact to your mind, say that word aloud. When the word is of no more interest, slide the paper down to reveal the next one.

When an image or inspiration comes, write a line or so about that image. Write as much as the word justifies and stop when the writing loses energy. All the while, allow no concern about time or expedience to interfere with this exercise. Should you go through the whole list without response, this merely means the level of your concentration is shallow. Your left brain is bleeding its concern into your creativity.

This is a good place to do the writing-channel exercise to deal with this right brain interference. Write down those thoughts coming into your concentration. Capture them on paper and then return to the first word and try again.

Writers with moderate and heavy problems with shifting

will use this exercise prior to writing an assignment at hand. It is a good warm-up procedure and initiates the right brain involvement needed to write further. Gymnasts and dancers warm up before a performance, and actors have rigorous regimes they use before meeting that first curtain.

Now for the list:

rotting figs	autumn
rubies on dark velvet	horse
dust swirls	crickets
a distant star	leather
red and yellow kites	rain
fresh bread	warm bed
funeral	cold night
cool hands	single pearl
pine	damp wood
leaves	candlelight
singing birds	nude
puppies	kiss
kittens	moss
rain	stone
playground	wood
laughter	speed
ocean	climbing
siren	anger
telephone	silk

You must also prepare for one of the fringe benefits from this exercise: Good ideas often emerge during this process. A single word or phrase can sometimes expand into something larger, be it screenplay or novel, short story or poem. The brain is vigorously involved and ideas come to the surface—such is the fun of image words. The writer may take them and run in all directions. A group of several writers may use the same word without a single duplication. Another time, there might be many with the same response to the same word.

Just writing a word is a way to initiate right brain participation. All words have a certain amount of visual energy, and this exercise focuses on that aspect. A better grasp of the power in words is managed as well. Part of the fun, too, is seeing how others responded to a given word. *Moss* is one we shall explore. The image it inspired was *spanish moss*, and the following adventure developed.

> *I see it hanging in that quiet corner of the forest. This is all that remains of the ancient ones who worshipped antiquity and prayed to the beards of their elders. Over the past centuries these hoary adornments have hung, waving silently to every whisper of the wind, continuing to live long past the demise of their owners. How strange, those sagacious old beards waiting for the return of the ancients. Yet, the tablets did prophesize this, and yonder's silent vigil is proof enough. I wonder, is it written that my own life's work will elevate me to this saintly state and my own white whiskers hang among the ancient ones? Seeking immortality?*

Observe how the real intent of the exercise is served as the writer is drawn into the reality of the fantasy that the writer himself created. This is how creative energy is generated and then perpetuated. Energy begets energy. In this way that enemy, writer's block, is inevitably defeated.

Another exercise that is fun and very helpful in showing how word power gives our statements cohesion is the "Exercise of Unrelated Statements." In this we take a list of statements and words that have no relationship to each other. Then we connect them with a sentence that makes the two unrelated thoughts make sense. Creativity is essential here; you also see how important it is to have a command of transitions. Begin with the first word, then use the list in its order. A sentence between each should make the list into a story.

Jesse James

Dodger baseball

Please, John, you're hurting me

Born April 4, 1883

Darn it anyhow

Hi, Nellie

Marsupials have pouches

Take the money and run

Kiss and tell

Now to show how the unrelated-phrases exercise can be solved, here is a sample:

Jesse James *seemed appropriately named when he became one of the best base stealers, in* Dodger baseball. *But Jesse was embarrassed when, in court, his neighbors testified that he abused his wife, whom witnesses swore they heard crying out:* "Please, John, you're hurting me." *It was not widely known that Jesse had been named for a grandfather, John Jesse James, a circuit court judge,* born April 4, 1883, *who was dubbed the "Ragged Judge" due to his coats being in tatters. Judge James's wife often complained about his appearance, but he just urged her to* darn it anyhow. *But no Jesse James story is complete without an account of his last game, in which he waved to his ex-wife and shouted,* "Hi, Nellie." *There had been no reconciliation, but as sure as* marsupials have pouches, *Nellie had taken her lawyer's advice to* take the money and run. *And when asked about her continuing relationship with James, Nellie insisted she could never* kiss and tell.

There is no denial of the mental gymnastics involved, but what a great feeling to put the pieces into place. It makes for greater confidence. The right brain has been pleasantly challenged, but the statements were eventually spliced into a plausible story.

Again, the blocked writer will find this and the other exercises helpful. The act of working with a creative challenge and sorting out words, organizing them into information, is fine medicine. You can create similar exercises for yourself by searching out unrelated statements from a newspaper. Try to make them as challenging as possible.

There is something about challenging one's creativity that benefits the state of our art. A Roman emperor proved this when one of his prophets was not able to come up with a prophecy. The emperor had him lowered into a cage of lions. The prophet had only to signal when his powers were returned. He was barely halfway down to the waiting beasts before he indicated that his grasp of prophecy had returned. From that time on he never again suffered such a lapse. His right brain, without question, was stimulated, because the prophecies fairly spilled from his lips.

There is an enormous amount of material stored in the brain. Experiences, impressions, lessons learned, observations—they all are there, tucked into convenient corners until called up for use. This is why you must never concern yourself about being smart enough to write. And this is the reason experienced writers urge admirers to write about what they know, what they might have stored in their brain waiting to become a part of a story. The problem writers have is one of access. Writers creating material from what they know will soar once they overcome the condition of blocked access.

A third exercise that can be useful is "Off the Wall," so named for lack of a better one. It is fun and interesting to explore. Much of its effectiveness comes from the amusement and utter foolishness it generates. A bit of humor must not be underestimated when dealing with creative access.

"Off the Wall" first appeared as a ghetto expression that identified a person of different personality, someone not weird, strange, or peculiar as much as incongruous; someone whose personality has a non sequitur quality. In slang terms, they rather bounce off the wall. "And the floor, ceiling, and even the door handles," a writer suggested.

Additionally, "Off the Wall" is original, provocative, and

charmingly fresh. It elicits that rare humor with a sense of oblique observation some writers have. Need it be said that schools or colleges can't provide for "Off the Wall" studies, though there is a constant search for means of bringing in new phrases and originality to relieve the tired old sayings and clichés that abound.

A curriculum committee writing a grant proposal for "Off the Wall—Freshmen and Sophomores" couldn't possibly bring much optimism to the task. Yet this exercise is not complicated: Think of a friend whose face and identity are well known to you. Then ask yourself, what do they smell like? Is there an identifying odor that could be associated with them? Now go a step further. Is there a flavor that might be associated with them? In other words, what do they taste like? Better yet, what flavor is their personality?

Obviously, here is a chance to use all five senses. Too much is written from the visual point of view, to the neglect of the other four senses. But each can apply in one way or another to some familiar person. Try it. Give someone you know an identifying smell, taste, sound, and texture. Do several of these to explore the range of your creative powers. The neglect of your use of the senses will show how to develop additional powers of description. A ginger girl with an applesauce smile might appear in your next story. That is "Off the Wall."

Textures are rare indeed in a lot of writing. It must come of our concern about touching each other. Accidentally lean against a companion—immediately the left brain flashes *don't* and we apologize. God forbid that we include touching in our writing. Give this some thought, because the inner writer is most eager to break some of the rules that inhibit us.

But on second thought, now that we have apologized, was that person smooth, soft, hard, rough, warm, or pleasant to touch? What texture did they have? Or better, what texture do they seem? Can you think of a corduroy person or two? A velour person? Have you ever known a silken personality?

In our writing classes, our comedian said his wife, blindfolded, could pick out his billfold from a lineup of fifty. To which she said, "Of course I could. His is the one rusted shut." That's not only funny, it's "Off the Wall."

In desperation for sounds, some writers attempt to write sound effects. This has an inherent danger in that the story tends to read like "Batman and Robin," with bangs, pows, sockos, and ouches. Avoid this. Capture the sound in descriptive prose; save the sound effects for special moments and then use them sparingly. Yet sound must be critical to the depth we are striving for. There are sounds that apply to some persons more than to others.

The effective use of sound is displayed by sightless persons using sounds to tell them when a traffic light has changed. There is a mechanism within the light that the blind are taught to listen for—that and the passing traffic. But think about applying sounds to the people around us. What does your wife sound like? Is there one identifying sound that applies to her? Or has your husband some sound more his than any other? Add sounds to that list of descriptions you have started.

One mother named her youngest son, the Faucet Drip Kid, because she could always tell when he left the bathroom: the water always dripped. This descriptive reality too often is absent in writing. In the years of radio broadcasting, the use of sound was something of an art. There was no picture to limit our imagination, but the sounds made our mind's eye alive. In films, the advent of sound spelled the end of careers for a lot of actors and actresses. Their voices were not always consistent with their appearances. The robust hero too often had a high, piercing voice, and the sultry actress unfortunately had a voice like Tugboat Bill.

In "Off the Wall" an unlimited range of descriptions awaits. Take the eyes, for instance. Why couldn't there be a texture or some imagined sound to them? To imagine this is right brain. Challenge yourself and explore the possibilities.

James L. Adams, in his book *Conceptual Blockbusting*, the art of "left-handed thinking," discusses creativity. Left hand, right brain; right hand, left brain—this is the scientific designation of hand to brain, since the nerve controls are cross-connected. The right brain responds to the left side of the body, the left brain to the right side.

The concept of applying the senses to other than their specialties (smell to sight) is left-handed thinking, and that means right brain. The book also shows how science benefits from creative, though unsubstantiated information:

> *The scientists who are responsible for breakthroughs in knowledge cannot operate entirely by extrapolating past (known) work but must utilize intuition too. Similarly the humanists who disregard the logical are doomed to be ineffectual (even counterproductive) in influencing social actions.*

This statement is important to both right and left brain thinkers. It means that progress is the result of specific information providing a springboard for intuitive or creative projections. Scientists are volunteering that advancement is due to intuitivity as well as to established fact. Creativity is indeed the cutting edge of advancement. Ironically, "Off the Wall" might well be a measure of advancement as well.

As a writing exercise, explore the usefulness of applying each of the senses to the function of the other. Write about tasting with your eyes, touching with your ears, hearing with your taste, seeing with your nose. Shift the various functions about to find out how much latitude there might be. The unrestricted use of "Off the Wall" here is deadly for wiping out writer's block. Whole areas of your imagination can be aroused, and this is incomparable in starting you to write.

Over the years there has been an interesting collection of identities born of "Off the Wall." There was Thunder Eyes, Sticky Winds, Hacksaw Smile, Man in the Chocolate Chip Hat, along with a long list of others.

After you have worked with this new tool for exchanging one sense for another, remember that there must be some judgment in writing as with any of the arts. Just as a fine chef will limit the amount of spice used in one recipe, so will the writer limit the temptation to stack up pages of chocolate dinosaurs and nutmeg voices. Use these devices at the most strategic times for the greatest effect.

For class entertainment, the handwriting exercise stands alone. A volunteer is asked to come forward and write his or her normal signature in longhand upon the blackboard. Usually the volunteer is a little apprehensive, not knowing what will happen. One woman who comes to mind was so rigid she resembled someone about to experience a root canal in the dentist's office. Told merely to sign her name, she relaxed a bit.

"Annadar" was the name she signed to her poetry, and she used it for the signature. Now she was told that in an earlier life she had been a respected Benedictine nun—Sister Anna of Benevolence. And that in this lifetime she had saved a whole village from starvation by leading a rescue party over the precipitous passes to the victims, who had been cut off by an avalanche. Then she was told, "Sister Anna, sign your name."

As she began to write her new name under the old one, there was a distinct quality of familiarity in both, but Sister Anna showed more dignity and seriousness. It showed to what extent she was thinking the part in order to express it in the signature. This is right brain, pure creative concentration. Her long consonants were subdued and the writing seemed to be at peace with itself.

Now Annadar was caught up in the fascination of becoming another person. She felt the right brain shift and later said it was as though there was an additional force directing her. Awareness of the class, she said, was lost. She was alone, her right brain dominant.

Annadar was then given another character, this time the

poor peasant daughter of impoverished country folk. They sold her as an infant to get food and shelter for fifteen brothers and sisters. In this character, Annadar was told how she had grown up in the foster family with servant status, regularly reminded of her lowly origin. She endured humiliation and brutality to a great extent and suffered extensive emotional damage.

"Your name is Scullery Ann," the volunteer was told. And as she listened to her life, she cringed visibly in keeping with the image forming in her mind. Her posture changed and so did her name, as it too illustrated the feelings of low esteem.

Her consonant stems were wizened, and there was no aggression in the form of her writing. It almost apologized for appearing. When asked if she were performing or honestly showing how she felt, Annador said she couldn't make that separation. In her mind it became real as she signed her name.

In keeping with the identifiers of a right brain state, our volunteer was amazed that nearly half an hour had passed since she came forward. Of course, in right brain there is no consciousness of time.

The last assignment for Annadar was meant to be a challenge. This one would be Anna Banana, the swingingest, most flamboyant hooker on Hollywood Boulevard. Miss Banana drove a velvet Cadillac—yes, one whose exterior was trimmed in white velour. And she wore the most outrageous gown ever to hang from a woman's body.

Interestingly, our volunteer grew visibly in height and obviously in imagined status. She grinned wickedly, then looped out a name with swirling panache. The class applauded as Anna rushed to her seat to make notes on the experience.

The Idea File

Again, farsighted Ray Bradbury must get credit for an idea. This time it's the idea file, which was mentioned once in a Bradbury lecture at the first Santa Barbara Writers' Conference in 1972.

Since then I have developed some variations of my own. To whom Bradbury is indebted for the idea will most likely be withheld until he writes *Son of the Martian Chronicles.*

An idea file is a simple concept, merely a plain manila envelope into which bits and scraps of paper are placed, each with an idea written on it. The beauty of an idea file is that it's a way of retaining those flashes of brilliance that come at the most inadvertent times. The wise person will stop, no matter what, and write down that idea, never waiting for a more convenient time.

No one can explain why ideas come when one is cutting the grass, washing dishes, scrubbing, defleaing the dog, grooming the cat, trimming toenails, showering, making love, thinking about making love, driving to the grocery store—the occasions are endless. The inconvenience of the moment might be an indication of the merit of the idea. Perhaps we have to be philosophical about the ill timing of ideas. One writer, for example, was known for bounding from the arms of her beloved to jot down an idea, begging his pardon for the interruption, then sheepishly returning to promise it would not happen again. She hoped.

That writer knew that were she so foolish as to not put down a good idea, she would never be able to find it when there was time to deal with it. Worst of all, she knew there might be a time when watching TV or the movies when there, before her eyes, would be her idea in living color. Someone else would have acted on her idea, that person becoming rich and famous and never needing another idea the rest of her life.

By now I estimate that the whole world has heard about my own experience with the idea file. Yet there might be some remote spot on the polar ice cap where my idea-file story has not been heard. And for the benefit of that small community, I will repeat it:

I was a reporter at the time and spotted a filler that caught my attention. For those who do not know, a filler is a line or two of obscure information about something regarding which you could not care less. The purpose of the filler is to pad out the vacant spots in a newspaper to make it seem chock-full of news. A typical filler might tell you, "Alaska has six trillion trees"—the interest here being that anyone cared enough to count them.

The filler that caught my attention was one that stated: Ninth century Vikings sailed as far south as the Mediterranean and returned with African slaves." I cut it out, then about four years later I found a second filler that stated there were colonies of black slaves in Ireland and Norway that were absorbed into the culture by the fifteenth century. With this the idea for *Black Viking* came to me; four years later it was a paperback original with Fawcett Books.

The point is to remember that ideas are a precious resource and we have to deal with them on their own terms. They are not definable or predictable; they merely *are*. When you need one they won't come. You go to the bathroom to brush your teeth and you get an idea. Nor can you think ideas. Worst of all, we writers are lost without ideas. This is the pure seed of energy from which a story develops. No writer, regardless of stature, can write a story without ideas. In structuring an outline on how to write a book, the idea is the first thing the writer has to have. Everything else falls into an order of progression.

Writers find themselves with idea donors from all corners. Shortly after *Black Viking*, a friend called to tell me about a terrific idea he was giving me for nothing. His idea was about a black warrior in Venice who was hired by a wealthy Venetian to shape up the army. The warrior did and became very popular. In addition, he fell in love with the merchant's frail but lovely daughter. They marry.

At this point it seemed I had heard this story before, but I listened politely as I was told further that there was a trouble-maker who kept putting doubts into the warrior's head about his wife's fidelity. Eventually the warrior went berserk and killed his wife.

"You have given me *Othello*," I told my informant. He looked puzzled for a moment, then grinned, realizing as I did that

Will Shakespeare had done a fine job with this idea. Writers also come to realize that all ideas are not the hula hoop or the Volkswagen.

Any number of attempts have been made to generate ideas using inspirational surroundings and carefully selected companionship. Bob Hutchins directed the Center for Democratic Institutions in Montecito, California, which cultivated some of the sharpest minds to be found. They had impressive sessions with world figures and any number of celebrity thinkers. But the center had little effect on either the world or its conditions. Neither smog, the Russian arms buildup, inflation, cellulite, nor dandruff were ever figured out or a means for controlling them decided upon. But the center did serve a very fine steak for lunch.

Some writers agree that ideas come from God, who spreads idea dust each evening. The ideas sift down about our heads like diamond chips. The fact that some of them come at inadvertent times makes me suspect that God has a great sense of humor.

A few of us are smart enough to grab a good idea when it comes our way. Others say, "That's a great idea, but I'm busy." This causes the idea to find someone else.

A bachelor writer in St. Louis said that he believes in grabbing ideas no matter what the occasion. He carries a pad for just that purpose. He is a thinking man, and each time he makes a conquest he explains early on to his lady that he has one peculiarity.

"I'm a writer," he explains. "We writers do strange things at times. Not funny-strange, just unusual. Like the times I have to dash to my memo pad to write down a certain item. When this happens it is nothing personal. I just make my living with ideas and they do come at unusual times."

This said, the fellow has smashing relationships. One of his companions was fascinated with his "idea thing." In a way she was puzzled because they really did come at unusual times. "It's as though they plan it," she said.

I never organize my own idea file. Each of the many envelopes I have filled with ideas contains something of a variety. This makes it surprising and exciting for me. I never know what I will find, and those times I am puttering, just sorting about the idea file gets me going.

Bradbury once said that sorting through his idea files was like becoming a mother bird. The ideas are like fledglings reaching their beaks out for recognition. "Me, me, me," they cry out, all wanting to become stories. Then the author laughs. "It gives me a grand sense of security to have more material than I can use in one lifetime."

ENTER
THE EDITOR:
LEFT BRAIN

The term *writing* is misleading. An act of creation, it includes a number of other skills that must be performed before it is complete. Editing, refinement, revision, rewriting, and reorganization—oftentimes over and over—also are part of writing. Nor does this account for hours of planning, research, and marketing that might be necessary before the book reaches the shelf. Still, when it all has come together, we toss it off as *writing*.

Writing, though, is only a part of the total performance. The major function to consider is *editing*. The brain must have been designed for writers, because it has two hemispheres. One is for writing and the other for editing. We create from the right and edit from the left. Without editing our writing would only exist in rough, creative, but less than effective condition. There would be nothing to resemble the polished prose we put between snappy dust jackets.

Remember, too—writing is bought by left brain institutions that prefer the polished product in preference to a less finished work of great potential.

The marketing director in a publishing house regards a new shipment of manuscripts with the cold eye of the packinghouse buyer appraising a load of baby beef. If this gives you the impression that publishers expect to make money, you are getting the idea. It costs money to manufacture books, so the industry seeks that writer who turns out the more finished work. And the difference is usually in the editing.

An editor is not like a writer. If editor and writer are the same person you have Jekyll and Hyde. The editor thrives on rules, regulations, guidelines, and specifics. Additionally, the editor needs a heart of granite.

In writing, grammar, spelling, organization, and syntax are

of little importance. But to the editor, these are the tools of the trade. And this does not mean the writer must dash out and acquire a degree in English. A knowledge of language and structure is obviously an asset. But being an avid reader has been found to be even more advantageous. The strong reading background provides a sense of correct grammar and an equally valuable feeling for story organization. Spelling is as close as your dictionary; a thesaurus is helpful too. A book of fundamental grammar is another good reference source.

Writing teachers usually agree that good writers started out as readers. Good editors must also be well read. There is a feel in good writing that is difficult to define. In one sense the editor listens for this; in a way, one might say that you experience good writing rather than read it.

With the right brain to create and the left to edit, one might be led to think that writing could become a matter of cranial mass production. If it were only that easy. The hemisphere performing needs to be dominant. The trouble is, they both like to be in charge, and just as the left brain whines to infiltrate the creative production of the right brain, right brain whimpers endlessly when the left side is editing:

> *Don't whack off that sentence!*
> *Wait, that was my best!*
> *Oh, no, you are cutting off that word?*

With all this in the background, the left brain works at refining and editing as the right brain struggles against the process. This is why writers find it difficult to edit their own work. They know it too well and forgive the errors and mistakes. It's like a mother with ten children who has to get rid of four of them. Which of her babies can she let go? Which of your words can you let go? And this is where the editor's heart of granite is useful. Being tough with your own work is hard to do.

One thing that helps is to let a bit of time elapse between

writing and editing. This tends to subdue our fondness for the writing and allows us to trim and revise as though it were a stranger's. Another thing that helps editing is to have an advance on the story and a publishing date to look forward to. By this time the publisher has read the story and gives some definite provision for revisions. Before this, the writer had to guess. The polite rejection slips we get do not contain much advice.

Newspaper work provides a chance to see both right and left brain types laboring for the common goal: deadline. Staff writers are pounding their research into information. Editors are going over it in critical fashion, cutting here and correcting there. Need it be said that editor and writer clash regularly?

The news editor's job is to ferret out any potential for libel, alienation of readership, and plain old mistakes. Their war cry is: "You writers make the copy breathless and we editors will make it make sense."

If newspaper editors sound hard-nosed, they are. They have to be in order to deal with outraged writers shouting, "You slashed the heart out of my story." Yet at day's end, both writers and editors might be found at the corner pub commiserating over the perils of deadline pressure.

Odd as this system may sound, it works. Writing and editing are adversary skills that complement each other. One is subjective and the other as objective as possible. Both work to produce the most information of greatest accuracy in the least amount of time. A good editor is one least involved with the writer or writing, who merely applies the rules for improvement.

Once a staff editor's wife was hired as a writer by the same newspaper. His colleagues kidded him about it. "What are you gonna do when you get your wife's story to edit?" one of the staff joked. And without even looking up from the headline he was writing, the editor said, "Give it to you."

A very good lesson can be learned here. The closer to home the writer and writing, the less effective the editor and editing.

Once again, this points out the difficulty in editing our own writing as well as an emotionally uninvolved editor might do it.

When writing stories where the source might be legally liable for what is said, authors must be certain that what they write is what was intended. A certain interpretation or change of version can occur in writing as well as speaking. When principals are quoted, they often complain about being misquoted. A wise editor will insist that reporters and writers have a taped interview of such sensitive sessions. It is common for a source to complain about being misquoted in a story, and when the taped interview is replayed the person always replies, "But that's not what I meant."

"But that's what you said," the reporter can respond, often with more than a little satisfaction.

We know what we intend to say, but in speaking, as well as in writing, it comes out differently. It seems the mind has a keen grasp of exactly what it wants to state, but the brain does not translate from words like the flowing sentences we see in sub-titled foreign movies. The mind visualizes images and impressions. Memory, observations, and information all pour into the transposition from image to expression.

Quite often we have to state two and three times the message we are attempting to portray in order to capture exactly what was intended. In writing we get to edit our words before sharing them, but in speaking we get no second chance. And often we say the wrong thing. Our intentions were admirable, but something was lost in the translation.

For this reason, the value of editing lies in the refinement it provides. Fine speeches are not spontaneous. They have been edited and refined, then mostly committed to memory. It's no secret that the public speaker who talks long enough off the cuff sooner or later will get one of his Florsheims caught in a cavity.

The first written version of any story is nothing more than raw copy. Editors refer to pages that have not been gone over as just that, "raw copy." It has not been flensed of errors.

In the years before the visual data terminals (VDTs) in news rooms, it was interesting to watch the reporter-editor exchanges during the busy time of the day. The reporter would complete a page of copy, read it for errors, make a pencil correction or two, and turn it in. An editor, usually some villainous type who loves to skewer hapless writers, takes it back.

"You wanna spell cat with two *t*'s today, ol' buddy?" the editor asks with a sardonic grin. The writer is mortified and snatches the pages to fix them.

"I've been rushed to keep a dental appointment," the writer explains lamely.

"What about here, where you use the same sentence twice?"

"Oh, that?"

Inside, the writer seethes for making such elementary errors, thus giving the editor reason to harass him. After all, the writer had such a vivid picture of what he intended to say.

But now the editor fires one final salvo. "I almost forgot," he says grinning. "You misspelled the mayor's name. But I fixed it for you, old top."

In spite of the baiting, some desk editor regularly saves a writer from making a fool of himself in public print.

Today, the cost of book publishing is so high that writers are expected to provide their own editing to a great extent. No longer are editing geniuses around to nurture the writer with a grand creative ability but lesser editing skill. Publishers make a final editing of everything before they go to print; they must for their own protection. But the writer is expected to submit highly refined manuscripts.

Contracts are offered on this basis, and new writers with editing deficiencies will find it tougher to break in. Learning to edit means learning an additional skill. It is not creative, which, in a way, can be a relief after 300 pages of right brain concentration. Equally important to know is that all fine writers are not fine editors. There are some of us who have trouble screwing down the mind to a level where each word is appraised, each thought sorted for refinement and brevity.

Kenneth Rexroth once said that editing was like searching your beard for fleas. Another writer in California said he exchanged editing with his wife, also a writer. This is a convenient arrangement, but there are inherent dangers. He told of one such instance when his wife came into his study with an icy expression on her face. "You ninny," she fumed. "You have effectively ruined one of the more eloquent sentences of my career."

The poor chap could only shrug and mutter that the sentence was a fine one indeed, but not appropriate for that part of the story. After that, he prayed for the phone to ring.

Intellectually, we writers know that editing is necessary. But emotionally, we resent it. Overall, editors have a convincing percentage of accuracy in their decisions. It demands so much more than correct spelling and grammar. The editor must have an ear for wrong words, awkward syntax, superfluous language, and still listen for the mood and voice of the writing. If it's a novel, point of view, conflict, and tense are only a few of the concerns. Clarity and consistency are additional responsibilities.

The editor will sometimes read a passage aloud, fitting the words to the ear. At other times there will be segments of a story that belong in a different place in the story and must be relocated. Thus, the editor must be a critical reader. To do all this demands a tough state of mind. And again one must wonder: How tough can I get with my own writing?

Another writer who exchanges editing with his wife said they worked out ground rules for their arrangement. They never discuss editing unless it is super-critical. And they never hand their work to each other, finding that when they slide it under the study door to the other, it is less personal. "And we remain married," both laughed.

A screenwriter who edits her own work said it is like removing your own tonsils—possible but painful. But the terms of her profession are such that there is no choice. She said that a few good books on basics such as grammar, structure, and fundamentals are all she relies on. Her most valuable asset is having been a voracious reader.

A number of fine books to bolster your editing skills are on the market. Most writers rely on a complete dictionary more than anything else. An Oxford English Dictionary is a boon to those who can afford one. It goes into detail about words and meanings, even word origins.

Another good book is one with guidance for style. The style of a piece of writing is the way the information is provided. Style makes the information uniform; for example, it means when one uses numbers throughout a manuscript, not spelling them out on one page and using numerals the next. This provides uniformity and simplifies the reading.

Another example of style is when mentioning the city, one should also give the state. There is more than one Memphis, Chicago, or Riverside. Using the state prevents confusion.

When editing, the elements of style must be considered at all times. A further example of style is when mentioning women. Are they called Mrs., Miss, and Ms.? Or are they called by their names, as when identifying a man? Whichever way, style means doing it the same way throughout.

Writers also ask, When do you edit a book or short story? Some write a page and then edit it. Others complete the full project, then edit it. There are many systems by which many writers will swear as being the only one. But with our present knowledge of right brain perception, we now have an idea of editing that is more compatible with the way the brain works. It demands a minimum of shifting from left to right.

The system works best when the writer has some form of outline. This way, segments of the story can be assigned each day as that day's allotment of work. The outline is the blueprint from which our story will be written, and therefore it is helpful in using the system.

As an illustration, assume that you are writing a mystery. You have reached the part of a story where the suspect is found with a smoking gun in his hand. That portion of the outline is marked off as the day's work. You flesh it out with research and creativity. When this is done, stop.

The amount of work in this assignment has been estimated as enough to fill the time you have in which to write. That day's writing should be all you attempt to do; when the designated amount of work from the outline has been done, stop, and go prune the roses.

To start the next day's work, begin by pencil-editing the work of the previous day. There are several advantages to this. First, the mind has had time to put space between it and the writing. There is less memory of what was written to interfere with the editing judgment. Second, editing the work from the previous day is an excellent way to review what has been said. The story, its characters and setting are thus renewed for the day's assignment ahead.

A novelist said that editing the previous day's work was similar to recapping a soap opera, which always begins by telling you something like, ". . . so Edna told Laurie that her recipe for marijuana brownies killed the cat Grandma loved so much she willed it a fortune in Iranian friendship certificates."

Pencil-editing is very helpful to the writer. Not only are corrections made, redundancies scratched out, and spelling lapses mended, the editor should make marginal notes to (himself) the writer when changes or explanations are needed. "Describes the weather," "Too long; trim back," are typical notations writers make in the margins when editing. As little as possible should be trusted to memory when either writing or editing. Make notes to yourself and even give praise when such is in order. The notation "Good fight scene" is helpful to the writer, even when you, the editor, are also the author.

All pages must be double-spaced. An amazing number of young writers are single-spacing their writing, which wastes time. The saving in paper is minuscule.

Editors have to write between the lines when pencil-editing; that calls for double-spacing. Publishing houses will not read single-spaced writing. It is murder to the eyes.

An edited page might appear as if a war was fought on its surface. There will be scratch-outs, memo balloons, marginal notes, and turkey tracks in general. But don't rewrite this on clean pages yet. Move on to the next day's assignment from the outline. Continue this system until the first draft of the work is done. Now you get to start all over again, first to rewrite the pencil-edited pages, including all the corrections and considering the memos.

Use this same procedure for writing a second draft. There will be fewer corrections, and the pages will be noticeably cleaner—sometimes. Also, when finishing this second draft, it's a good idea to take a break. Get some space between your mind and the story. Take this time to patch up the friendships that have eroded because you have been writing and were too busy to call or visit. Do your yard work or go fishing.

After several days to several weeks have passed, give the story one more writing. This will be the third draft, and though the pages are somewhat clean, errors and corrections will still be possible. The space of time might reveal a structural weakness that did not appear before. Third draft is also a time when the first page is established. Polishing and revising that first page is third-draft work. It's wasteful to do so at an earlier time, because the story might decide it needs a different first page.

This system works because it uses the essence of editing to supplement the writing. With each draft, editing and rewriting combine to improve our stories. And let's face it, most of us are three-draft writers.

There will always be someone who claims to write perfect first pages, but don't believe it. First-draft people are either braggarts or just kidding themselves. A wise senior editor once said, "Show me a first-draft manuscript and I'll show you room for improvement."

During the 1920s and 1930s, known as the golden era of American publishing, the book industry took on more of the editing load for its writers. Rough copy was accepted by publishers when interesting potential was found in that writing. This was the time when some of the giants of literature were producing: Ernest Hemingway, Thomas Wolfe, F. Scott Fitzgerald,

Gertrude Stein all were aided or developed by an editor who stands out like the Christmas star.

Maxwell Perkins was that editor, a man with the gift for making authors successful by editing their work to its most effective level and supporting them, financially and emotionally, when they were between projects. Perkins saw promise in chaos, and some of the most popular books of the time were developed under his guiding hand. Editor and eventually vice-president of Charles Scribner's Sons publishing for thirty-six years, Perkins has been called one of the greatest literary influences of all times. He preferred anonymity to the celebrity he made possible. His instincts were remarkable and he regularly put his position with Scribner's on the line in the cause of some unknown writer he believed in. Thomas Wolfe was a notable example.

In A. Scott Berg's biography of Maxwell Perkins, Berg tells how the man took reams of Wolfe's pages, which filled a box, and patiently worked over them, organized them, and mapped out refinements. The result was *Of Time and the River*, said by some critics to be the finest example of the novel written in America.

Perkins the editor was something out of a writer's dream. He loaned his authors money, made arrangements for their travel accommodations, and listened to their troubles like a father. Even for that period, Perkins was an exception, although publishers then did go out of their way to assist their writers.

Another example of Perkins's dedication was F. Scott Fitzgerald, who languished in France, mulling over one of his novels as Max Perkins kept him afloat with regular advances. Although their debts are known, it would be difficult to measure how much Hemingway, Wolfe, Fitzgerald, Ring Lardner, Erskine Caldwell, James Jones, Taylor Caldwell, and a roster of others owe the man.

Today, undiscovered talent still abounds, and there are writers who might someday become the Caldwells, Lardners, and Hemingways of this period if another Max Perkins could magically appear.

But such is not the case. Writers now are forced to lie awake with visions of celebrity hovering over their heads. We know we must write with clarity and simplicity, trimming and pruning for greatest effect. We know that in order to write effectively we must edit effectively—without much help.

"You expect me to become two people," a young author howled. "First I have to love my stuff to pieces and then you want me to tear it to shreds."

Correct. As certainly as the blacksmith pounds and heats his steel to near melting, then plunges it in water to quench the heat, so must the writer-editors shape their own work. This is the hardening process that brings metal to maturity and changes it into steel. Through fire and quenching, pounding and shaping, the impurities are purged and the product takes on that keen edge the Damascans perfected a thousand years ago in weapon making.

A colleague, Jack Smith, columnist for the Los Angeles *Times*, said that when he worked at the copy desk as a rewrite man, he would create wonderful pages, then watch the editors read them, laugh, and proceed to cut them to bits with blue pencil slashes.

Though the professional editor is made to sound terribly hard, he or she still has a feeling for potential. It is not uncommon for an editor to attach a note to the rejected work of some promising writer, saying: "We would like to see anything else you might have, although we do not have a place for your current novel."

This is known as a "glowing rejection," and writers who get one should feel they have a toe in the door. There is an element in publishing that has nothing to do with editing, writing, or ideas. It has to do with timeliness. Writers have no control over this. If we could fathom the formula for timeliness, the road to Las Vegas would be overflowing with authors rushing to gamble to make millions—not write books.

Timing is such a factor that an agent once said, "If the Bible had not been written and some new writer came up with something called the New Testament, some senior editor would reject it with an apologetic note: 'Sorry, we are not publishing Jewish tragedies.' " The only answer is to keep writing.

Back to editing. There are some writers who may never effectively edit their own work. Some of us are so right brain that working any length of time in left brain is nearly impossible. Even Hemingway, Perkins observed in his memoirs, never did sort out "who" and "whom." Nor are all the popular writers today first-line editors of their own material.

It is possible to find an editor or someone with editing skills who is available for consultations. They might even work on commission if the writing is impressive. Good writers are scarcer than good editors, because editing can be taught.

Don't be intimidated. Even today, publishers will consider some tremendous piece of work if the market is tempting enough—and will provide the editing. Publishers are in business to make money. If your writing has promise—and you have done all you possibly can to improve it—send it off. Use the *Writers Market* lists. Remember, too, the rule is, query first.

There are rumors that publishing house editors are deceptively human, that they are actually eager to find something outstanding in the mounds of editorial shale the postal service dumps on their desks. Just as an oil driller or a miner prays to strike it rich, so much an editor feel when he attacks a new stack of manuscripts. "When I reach into the pile," an editor on panel discussion at the Santa Barbara Writers' Conference said, "I pray that the Big One is here somewhere."

In this same discussion editors were asked about their feelings on first-page impact and its importance. They said that quite often (sometimes 90 percent of the time) they know they will reject within the first few pages, often by the first page. Writers are fools, they said, if they don't polish their first pages.

It is not uncommon for writers to write a first page fifteen to twenty times before they are satisfied. In my own experience, I have done first pages nearly thirty times, and when the book was published I wished I could have one more chance at that first page. Conversely, as Perkins said, there is a time when the writer must give up the pages and send them in. With each revision some of the original juice is wrung out. The writer must stop or else the flavor is lost.

Max Perkins said, in the book by A. Scott Berg, that Hemingway admitted revising parts of *A Farewell to Arms* about fifty times. "Before the author destroys the natural qualities of his writing," Perkins stated, "that's when the editor has to step in. But not a moment sooner. . . ."

In considering the high rate of rejected material versus accepted work, an editor guessed that only about 2 to 5 percent of the submissions sent to her publishing house were accepted. She also said that an inordinate number of writers have no idea what publishers want.

"Too often," she continued, "writers tackle subjects about which they have little or no knowledge or experience." Her advice was, "Write about the things you know about; things you find interesting or have experienced. It's difficult to fake expertise," she said.

In creative writing classes we worked out a list of items writers should keep in mind when editing their work.

Consistency. Edit with consistency in mind so the story does not wander from present tense to past, the left-handed suspect does not suddenly become right-handed. Or the suspect who leaves in a red Buick does not return in a blue Pontiac. These are only a few examples of inconsistency editors have to deal with.

Live in the Dictionary. If you are even slightly unsure of a word's meaning or spelling, reach for the dictionary. Make this a reflex habit. Keep a dictionary within reach when typing and use it at the drop of a consonant. Anyone whose dictionary is not well worn either is too smart to be a writer or too lazy.

Editors Are Listeners. Read the work you are editing as though you are a publisher who is wondering, "Do I want to pay this writer fifty thousand dollars for this manuscript?" In order to read intensively, read aloud to better feel the sound of the words, the characters, and the setting. Listen to the writing and be patient. Editing is a slow process.

Simple Sentences. The best and most effective sentences are clear and simply crafted. Do not get too far afield from the old-fashioned one-thought sentences which are highly efficient when a moment of denouement is at hand. At this critical time in a story the reader must not be lost; the simple progression from one thought to the next is imperative.

Simplicity and clarity are important to effective writing and indispensible for editing. Robert Gunning wrote a fine book on the subject, *The Technique of Clear Writing*, which should make professional and beginning writers take a second look at their work. After a succession of printings, the book is still to be found on the shelves. Among its provisions are these principles of clear writing:

- Keep sentences short—on the average.
- Prefer the simple to the complex.
- Develop your vocabulary.
- Put action into your verbs.
- Use terms your reader can picture.
- Tie in with your reader's experience.
- Write the way you talk.
- Make full use of variety.
- Write to express, not to impress.*

*The principles cited here are slightly different from those in *The Technique of Clear Writing*. They are adapted from *How to Take the Fog out of Writing*, by Robert Gunning and Douglas Mueller,© 1981 by Gunning-Mueller Clear Writing Institute, Inc. Used by permission.

The Gunning method has been extensively used in commercial and business seminars where clear writing is critical to career advancement. In the world of advertisement, clarity is a watchword.

In regard to action verbs, it should be understood that we are not talking about the active voice as opposed to the passive voice. We mean that active verbs should not be exchanged with action substitutes. The action substitute is becoming so common that the reader tires of everyone in a story "plunging" into a chair—no one seems to merely sit. They dash, bound, stride, and canter about—but rarely walk. A few pages of this and the reader, not to mention the editor, is exhausted. Eventually, assuming the reader as well as the editor finishes the story, it is delightful when someone *opens* a door or *has* a drink instead of "tossing it down." Some restraint must be used with action substitutes, although they are effective at moments of suspense or emotion. The technique must not be abused lest the reader develop an immunity to it.

As the editor works to develop and improve, there will in time be moments of new power. A mediocre sentence now glows. The important thought that was buried in two pages of prose now reposes in a few crisp sentences that are as incisive as rapier thrusts. With the passing of time and gaining of experience, and most of all with patience, you can see fine stretches of rewarding results.

As an editor, you might not get equal recognition with the writer, but you know that the writer would not be possible without you.

A final item of editorial importance to consider is the fact that language constantly changes. The contemporary use of some terms may now have a different meaning. Editors must read enough to be up-to-date and know the current meanings of words whose definitions are changing or changed.

An amusing example of word change was shared one evening when a writer was reading from a revised science fiction novel. The scene she read was one that took place when a space crook was robbing a wealthy moon baron. The line was: "I can't allow you to take my family jewels." After this there was an impressive pause before she said, ". . . then the baron wailed and clutched them tightly."

The author had overlooked the common popular use of "family jewels," which had become a common term for male genitalia. She assured us, after order was restored, that the merchant would survive and she would alter the language.

Jim Quinn, author of *American Tongue and Cheek,* points out that even the literary immortals have sometimes lost touch with the vernacular. They too made these same errors and also suffered lapses; Quinn's example was Walter Savage Landor, who was negligent in his use of the word *twat,* a usage, Quinn observed, that made "Pippa Passes" (1v, "Night" 292–295) a favorite with graduate English students:

> *Then, owls and bats*
> *Cowls and twats*
> *Monks and nuns, in a cloister's mood*
> *Adjourn to the talk-stump pantry!*

Quinn notes that the Oxford English Dictionary lists *twat* (erroneously or disingenuously) as "low obsolute" [sic] and says that Robert Browning erroneously used the word "under the impression it denoted some part of the nun's attire." This was apparently because of "Vanities of Vanities" (1660), where Browning read:

> *They talk't of his having a Cardinalls Hat*
> *They'd send him as soon an old Nun's Twat.*

With all respect to Robert Browning and his place in literature, it would seem that by his example the writers of today must keep an ear tuned to the language. Of course, if Browning had been able to find an effective editor, this gaffe could not have occurred for all eternity to ponder and cluck about. Nor would the feeling of writer fallibility we all share. It did happen, though, and for that reason we can feel akin to those literary greats who left a few muddied footsteps along the way.

Review

Some phases of editing will be more important to one writer than to another. We won't all need the same warnings and guidelines. The various elements of editing may be used to repair errors and improve the work. You are urged to list the examples in Chapter 5 that are most helpful to you and your needs. By using a list, the elements of editing you feel are important will be before you as a reminder.

A Suggestion

First-Page Impact is something all writers must take into consideration during the editing process. As intensive reading and editing progress, you will find parts of your writing that are very impressive. This might be the most advantageous place to start the story. When you find a dynamic sentence, give some thought to putting it on page 1, Chapter 1.

Exercise

An editing exercise should give you practice and experience. The following exercise may be done on someone else's writing, not your own. That way there will be fewer pangs about cutting or revision. *This is a homework assignment:*

> *The opportunity to look over a professional editor's shoulder as he trims, revises, and proofs is an informative one. And the next best thing is to take some published article and take it apart, use its facts, and rewrite your own version of the original. First, under-*

line the facts. Then list them to use when you begin writing. Take the original page out of view or hide it from sight. Now, from your notes, create a version of the original story.

When you compare this with the original version, you will see why certain things were done and will understand the tactics involved in setting up an article.

This is a good way to realize that writing and editing are nothing more than an endless Scrabble game in which bits and pieces of information are pieced into something that comes out as The Story. The experienced editor is an X-ray machine seeing more than the flesh of a story—the editor sees the bones and fittings as well.

Suggested Reading

Effective Writing, by Robert Hamilton Moore. Holt, Rinehart and Winston, 383 Madison Ave., New York, N.Y. 10017 (1955).

The Oxford English Dictionary (bookstore or library).

Associated Press Style Book. The Associated Press, 50 Rockefeller Plaza, New York, N.Y. 10020.

The Random House Dictionary. Ballantine Books, A Division of Random House, New York, N.Y. 10022.

Published in paperback, this dictionary is a 1,073-page compilation of word-use information. Its back section has the signs, symbols, and elements of style writers and editors use and exchange.

TELLING
THE STORY

The ability to write is one skill, to tell a good story is another. All writing does not contain a good story, nor are all effective stories in writing. We must think of the story as an independent element that first appears in the mind and then mingles with writing images that flow from the fingers onto paper. If the mix of writing and story is good, you are successful.

The late Senator Everett Dirksen of Illinois was a man who told great stories. But during a senate filibuster, his command of language mingled mellifluent words into sentences meaning nothing. Mr. Dirksen's words had become a political weapon, though they told no story. Elegant, yes, but empty.

A lot of writers are like this; they take the story for granted, as though it and writing came canned like bean and bacon soup. But good stories must emit from the right brain, and for this reason, writers now comfortably at one with their right brain must take a closer look at the story.

Ask yourself, does my story idea have good potential? Does it convey a message or provide new information? Some stories have more possibilities than others, so writers must be selective in deciding which ones to write.

The good story is an elusive combination of words that convey conflict, information, interest, and revelation. Finding all this, we next must know how to tell this story in the most impressive fashion. And here is where the champions rise to the top like country cream. No one will argue that the fine storyteller can spin a second-rate yarn so well the listeners won't know the difference.

To do this, the writer needs a solid knowledge of story construction and what works to the best effect. This comes with experience and work. Stanislavski, the Russian dramatist, said that the finest playwrights need to have written many bad plays to rise to acclaim.

Evaluating a story is especially difficult when it's your own story. But one of the surest ways to examine a story that is not working is to go back to the outline. If you have a novel, for example, and it does not work, the outline will show the weakness much more clearly than the manuscript. Here is your idea in its barest concept, without the embellishment of words to diffuse scrutiny. If there is a lack of conflict in the story, there will be none in the outline. If there is a need for adventure and suspense in the story, it will be caused by there being no provision for it in the outline.

A story is no better than its outline, as surely as we humans are no taller or shorter than our skeletons. Our bones are the outline of our structure. The same is true of our skeletons of composition. Why else do editors ask for an outline with two chapters of your query submission? The chapters show your writing, but the outline reveals the potential of your story. As a result, the strong writer with a weaker story idea will have a better chance.

One of the most criticized points of any story is the beginning. The reader who declares, "I hated the ending," had to read the whole story to get there. The reader who hates the beginning is not likely to buy the book.

Feeling and critical opinion are established by this first page. This would indicate that a strong start is very much in order. But "strong" need not be confused with a car over the cliff or a bludgeon across the noggin in the first paragraph. Strong means getting the reader's (editor's) attention. Curiosity is a useful tool. Why else do so many magazine features begin with a question:

"Did you know it's possible to make a million dollars in your own home?"

"Would you like to be a centerfold girl at age eighty?"

"What are the chances of your poodle becoming a man-eater?"

No matter how remote the question, it gets your attention. Another technique to consider is an established belief by some novelists that the effective story begins as close to the ending as possible. Beginning early in the story is most convenient for the writer, but not always the most interesting for the reader.

Other writers start with some strong inner action and use the flashback technique. Their stories often read like news headlines: "City Hall Gambling Found." This said, we read on to find out what happened. Once the reader has something to chew on, the writer can tell a bit of background material. It's like telling the story inside out.

But the writer must also use judgment. The story might not need to be told from the inside out. Those stories with a lot of information, mystery, and excitement are sometimes best told from the very beginning. There are no slow places, and this simpler form is not only easier to read, it is easier to write.

A story is like a baby: Its infancy is most interesting to the new parents. But everyone else is not that enthralled with diapers and those precious first steps. So it is with the reader. Until a story develops personality and gets into trouble and finds adventure, it's not that interesting. Of course, there are some exceptions, as always. Some of us have had fascinating infancies. In that case our stories are best told from that earliest time.

So how do I know where to begin? asks the puzzled young writer. First, you can't possibly know where to begin until you have finished the first draft. Beginnings are like titles. You start with a working title, but quite often the story can change enough so the original title is no longer appropriate. So it is with beginnings as well.

An example of a story that starts with the beginning is the film *Shane*, from the novel by John Schaefer. It begins with the star, Alan Ladd, riding into the story from the distant foothills and ends with him riding out of town from the other end.

By contrast, remember the film with Ava Gardner and Humphrey Bogart, *The Barefoot Contessa,* which starts with her graveside services, Bogart standing there in his trenchcoat, rain dripping from his fedora. In this case the story is done in clever flashback sequences.

Generally, simple stories with heavy action are best told chronologically. There are fewer twists of complicated intrigue, but much sequential action. These stories work because of their simplicity.

At the other end of the spectrum we have the difficult plot with much introspection and intrigue. Some details are withheld until later to establish the greatest effect. The reader's attention is held with elements of mystery, and mystery is nothing more than the absence of information.

Because the first page is critical to storytelling, your right brain will never serve you better than in the initial paragraphs, where you entice the reader into your story with the most imaginative seduction possible. In fact, having decided on the place to begin their story, some writers will construct a detailed outline just for the first page or so.

The word *seduction* is not only important to the manuscript, it is important to the outline. This quality must be evident at an early point in order to direct its forces into the story. Seduction is highly visible in a bookstore. Study the browsing readers and observe how they pick up a book and read the first few lines. If they turn to the next page, the writer has effectively seduced that reader, and the chances that he or she will buy book are improved. *Reader* is an all-important word as the writer writes *for himself,* but *to the reader.* After all, the story travels from the writer's brain into the reader's.

Read has become such a common term among editors that it has become a noun when applied to the quality of a story. A good *read*, to an editor, means a story of high quality. In discussions it will be said that the *read* of a certain story is its greatest asset. The word is important for writers to remember. Editors have this in mind as they decide whether or not "this story is right for our lists."

Some stories are tougher to begin than others. But with all the information at hand, and the need to find that elusive "right" place to start, the right brain invariably comes up with something that works. Just think aloud, "What is the first thing I would like to say in this story?" Then weigh this against, "What is the first thing the reader should know about this story?" When your answer satisfies both questions, that's where you start.

With a workable beginning established, the story should seduce the reader into continuing. To sustain interest, the writer must unfold enough plot to add momentum, develop the visible characters, and reveal some interesting segments of background. The inexperienced writer can lose that reader after a commanding start. A tip to remember is not to be stingy with details at this point.

The strong start has introduced the reader to a moving current that sweeps him or her into the story. Generous helpings of plot, character development, and background are the critical ingredients of our formula. As this happens, an effective story emerges.

During the writing process, as the story unfolds, the writer has no means of perspective. The painter can move back a few steps from a watercolor to better view the work, but the writer is inside the story. It is almost impossible to step back because the story is as much in our brain as it is on the pages.

A series of checks for establishing perspective has been provided by Robert Hamilton Moore, a chairman of composition at George Washington University. Dr. Moore's book, *Effective Writing*, lists the vital fundamentals for retaining perspective during a writing project. There are five of them:

Significance. With the author's purpose in mind, how important is this book?

Newness of Materials. The approach to, or grouping of, the material and its conclusions.

Accuracy of the Facts and reasonableness of the inferences based upon them.

Scope of the book. How completely does it cover its topic, considering the author's purpose and audience?

Readability is closely related to clarity but is not identical with it. The first four points deal with content of the book. The last two are related to style.

These five fundamentals apply to both fiction and nonfiction. But for our purposes here, let us condense them. The right brain works best with fewer rules, so the previous five will now become three:

Readability means our pages not only have clarity but a style of writing that embodies more of the conversational voice.

Information means the writing presents new ideas and often a challenge the readers might not have considered before.

Good story means the writer has a clear idea where the plot is heading and thus gives the reader the most satisfaction possible. New and interesting material is needed as well.

Readers, editors, and publishers cherish these qualities. Whenever they find them they invariably sit down to read the pages. Of course, there are exceptions, like the coffee table buyers who select books with jacket colors that don't clash with the drapes.

The need to use a conversational tone is also important to storytelling. There is something about writing that causes some people to change personality. An example is the letter you get from a witty friend who never fails to amuse you. But in a letter, the voice is changed. The language seems lifted from some English term paper:

> *Dear Mike:*
>
> *I take this moment, pen in hand, to write and say hello. I am fine. I hope you are fine, too. The folks are fine and I'll bet yours are, too. There is not much to do today so I am writing to you.*

Where, you wonder, is that funny, entertaining person you remembered? The answer is simple. He is using his book-report voice from American Lit, the most recent pattern he has for writing.

We all have an assortment of voices. Another example is the receptionist called Old Battle-Axe at work. Her colleagues would be amazed to hear her at home, where her sweetie-pie tone is totally out of character with the office image. Nor could you convince her husband that at work she is something of a desk sergeant.

By concentrating on our most natural voice, our right brain is assured that things are well and nonthreatening. The left brain will activate at the least sign of danger or stress. But the calm, conversational voice gives no reason to be alert, and the right brain can function with creative impunity.

For this reason, some writers are alcoholics. They know by experience that their creativity remains in force when they are more or less calm and can write with a conversational tone. The problem is that writing while snockered may cause the writing to sound the same way. It's quite possible to write with an alcoholic slur.

There is a good exercise for writing with your conversational voice. Talking aloud as you write this assignment is one of the requirements. You are asked to write two pages about a simple dot (·), with no guidance other than to study the dot for a moment, then as you talk aloud, put down the thoughts that come to your mind. There will be questions, but merely ignore them. Just do it. Stop reading at this point and begin. As you do, your right brain will be licking its chops.

Resistance to this exercise is predictable. You are too used to having a lot of guidelines with assignments. But anything you do on this assignment will have had to come from your own creativity. If it's one line or hundreds, they are all yours.

What can I write about a dot?
This makes sense?
Is that all?

Each is one of many questions writers ask when confronted with the dot and nothing else. But the only advice is to write whatever comes to your mind and let it happen. In class, its interesting to see the slow transformation into right brain that takes place. There is something fascinating about this transformation. The eyes focus into the distance, and facial expression is one of deep contemplation, and an obvious detachment takes over. Some will make a few notes in a somewhat different fashion; a few will grin devilishly, as though to say, "Okay, wise guy. You want dots, you are getting dots."

Expanding a speck of ink into something comprehensible is pure creativity. Best of all, right brain exercises are fun because they are escapist. Sharing the results with others in class is also fun, as a few of the following will show.

The authority on the East and the Himalayas wasted no time establishing his dot in home territory—the officer's club at Katmandu. Our authority began:

> *It was deucedly humid sitting that morning with the paper, staring at the first dot on the first page. This speck was more than a period; it contained my coded orders from Central Headquarters. To the eye there was no perceptible difference from the others on the page. But when put under my scope, there was the micro-dot of information that might conceivably change the balance of power about the world.*

The humorist was equally adept at locating the assignment with convenience for his best voice:

> *They mostly called her Dorothy, this older sister of mine. But I always called her Dot. She was small, round, and insisted on having the final word. Yes, Dot suited her to a T.*

Another writer we shall identify as the Wise Guy began his story by describing a police lineup where a little old vegetable lady stared at a row of hoodlums and toughs who were standing under the lights. One of the men was an assailant. The vegetable lady had to identify him.

> *"I don't know," she began, scanning the row of rowdies one by one. Then she paused. "Wait," she shouted and pointed at a fellow with shredded cuffs bagging about his ankles. "Dot's the one," she called out, "Dot's him, all right."*

In each assignment there is the possibility of a story becoming visible. That's how stories are born. A few words appear and then a few more, until a message or statement is apparent. The assignment calls for undiluted right brain expression. There is no way to develop an accumulation of words into a creative statement without using the right brain.

Remember how each writer took the subject to the most comfortable territory possible? Artists dislike change because they know from experience that they work best in familiar surroundings.

Ask any experienced writer *where* you should write and you will be told to write where you feel most comfortable. Ask that same writer *what* you should write about and you will be told to write about those things and places you know best. Unless you keep this in mind, your writing will be just another grain of sand on the beach of ambition.

"But it just sounds too simple," writers have been known to complain. This is their left brain speaking. It has learned from advanced algebra that the tougher the solution the greater the reward. Like the old teamster who mixed a pinch of alum with his horses' grain, then took one himself—he felt that anything that tasted so bad must be great for your health. Think what it did to the germs.

If writers were given an algebraic equation that would make them successful authors and it were;

$$X = 2(WE^3 - 3BX - R^1) + (4Y \times E^9) = SUCCESS$$

this would be acceptable. Anything so abstruse has to be good, is that line of left brain thinking. The difficult equation is more compatible with our educational background.

Even though we are told by experts to trust our instincts, resources, and feelings, it sounds too easy. Of course, no algebraic equation ever published a novel or short story, but we are more inclined to put our trust in them.

The left brain covets the Ph.D., while the right brain prefers a sunset. For those of us feeling our way into right brain perception and applying those perceptions to serious application, to do so is contrary to just about everything we have learned in life. And here is the elusive handle to evaluating a story: The good story gives you a good feeling; the bad story doesn't. Not exactly the rules for playing the stock market, but writing is worlds apart from Dow Jones.

For new writers as well as those who are floundering about, the answers are in your right brain. Listen for them and trust them. They are familiar because you hear them in your natural voice.

"Write about those things you like, know about, and have the most interest in learning," said the late Kenneth Rexroth to a gathering of writers. Rexroth was one of the few remaining links with literature's golden era of the twenties and thirties. Translator, poet, and philosopher, he said further, "If you do this you will have more stories than you can complete in several lifetimes."

In summary, we have been urged to improve our storytelling because good writing does not guarantee effective prose. We must work on the beginnings of our stories. In doing this, our work will *read* well. And if we have used our most natural conversational voice, our way will be much easier. All of which brings us back to confront that recurring word: trust. Our feelings, instincts, and most natural abilities deserve our trust.

Write from your own point of authority, because when you are writing, if you have done your homework, you are the authority. This belief is just another term for confidence.

"I'd rather be confident than correct," a writer once said over a martini one evening.

"Not me," a colleague replied. "I'd rather be interesting than accurate."

If both positions were distilled they would mean the same thing: Facts change with time, but interesting writing is forever.

Review

This chapter is meant to emphasize the relationship of storytelling to effective writing. You should now turn back to the beginning of this chapter and make notes of those points that relate to your own writing. Ask yourself:

Is this my most natural voice?
Do I work on my beginnings?

Is my writing a good read?

Are parts of it seductive?

A reminder: Read your writing aloud to "see" it more clearly.

Exercise

Use the "dot" assignment as a guinea pig. Write one of your own, then decide if your version starts at the most effective place. Is there another part that might be stronger for a start? Write your version of the dot with an inside-out beginning. Then do another with a start from the earliest beginning. Compare the two. Is the chronological version better or weaker?

Describe in words the tone of voice in your assignment. Is it a voice you recognize? Identify where and when you most use this tone of voice. How might it be improved? As you find answers, write them down and evaluate them.

Is there ample description in your dot assignment? Be tough on yourself and write what you think and feel about your pages. Remember, better writers don't just write about a car, they describe a two-door sedan with faded paint. They have characters with freckles and small feet, slender fingers, warts. Readers love details, which remind them of people they know, allowing them to identify with your story.

What is the intent of your story? Its message? Does it have background and dimensional people, places, and things? Did you rush putting the story together or were you patient in assembling the many pieces? Ask yourself these questions and answer them as honestly as possible–in writing.

Suggested Reading

There are many examples of good writing with effective stories to use as models. Analyze these stories as you have your own. Search for defects that might have escaped the writer and editors.

It happens all the time. Read a few passages of Joan Didion's writing and William Faulkner's. Take a library break and spend a morning browsing the better storytellers. Find a Truman Capote book and one by Eudora Welty. Read and listen to their storytellers. Compare what you find with your own work. This is a very good way to isolate your weaknesses. Best of all, you will find a lot of things you are doing correctly.

WRITING:
THE HOLISTIC
APPROACH

There are times when a writer feels that a piece of work seemed to write itself. This is not imagined, it is a level of concentration we have when body, mind, and spirit are in harmony. Though we are often prone to attribute our success to external conditions, creative achievement comes from within.

One of the worst mistakes writers make is distrust their own minds. Believe in your brain power; trust your thoughts. This is not easy to do in some cases because one of the left brain conditions in education is that of making the student feel inferior. This way the instructor can pretend that he is God, that he has control, and that his word is all-important. But this is not reasonable thinking. Your mind is as much God as the instructor's. As writers we only have one mind to use. We cannot go to the instructors and ask to borrow theirs.

The important message to be found in holism, a study of separate units that are equal to or greater than the whole, is that it teaches us to use and respect our own facilities. For many gifted aspirants, to believe in their own resources is too much of a barrier to overcome.

Writers must realize that we are like castaways in a sea of uncharted distances. But we have a compass: our personal creative energy. All the answers lie within our own holistic combinations. Our body, our mind, and our spirit are imbued with natural wisdom. What does that mean? It means you should use your body, your mind, and your spirit. Believe in them and your own instincts and they will serve you. Trust yourself.

In my own experience as a news reporter and columnist, I can look back on that time as one of frustration. I was searching for something more than momentary glimpses of creative ability.

My writing confidence usually eluded me. I wondered why those glimpses came and just as quickly left.

A moody editor could make a cutting remark, the system could remind me of my tenuous position, and there would go my creative perception. At the same time my free-lance work at home was suffering too, and this bothered me because it had been my survival kit.

I was a man in search of himself. I would run on the beach and ponder the problem. I would drive to work and worry about it. What was I looking for? I had no idea until one morning as I sat writing the routine boilerplate that goes with newspaper work I realized: No exterior force will ever help me. I must rely on my own *inner energy*.

For all writers this must become a shibboleth. The power and inspiration we seek comes from within. Here is the initial rule for establishing a functional holistic state.

Begin with your body. For me, walking, running, exercise, and weight lifting put me in closer touch with my body. Soon, the seductive hand of journalism was less important to me. I was centering on my own resources by acknowledging that I needed to take better care of myself.

As I developed a feel for a more holistic existence, I still had no name or definition for what I was experiencing. All I knew was that my writing was suddenly improved, along with my state of mind.

It is ironic that one day when browsing in a bookstore, I picked up a cookbook—a holistic cookbook. Its introduction was a revelation. Here it was, the message of body, mind, and spirit. I had been reaching for a holistic existence without even knowing it.

Bookstores can provide you with a number of good books on the subject. Read about, more than discuss, holism. You will find that some of your colleagues will question this "holy-ism" business you are interested in. The practice of holistic balance has nothing to do with traditional religion. It merely means using and relying on your own systems.

In the East the value of yoga, meditation, Asian martial arts, Tibetan thought control, all are relative to achieving proper balance. Learning to believe in your native assets is relative to applying them to writing. The writer must withdraw from as much of the left brain world as possible—at least when working.

The urgency of the word *trust* will continue to appear throughout these pages. Through trust the writer finds confidence and turns inward to untapped powers with which we all were born. Such practice has been used by the ancients for centuries. In India the word for one's inner force is *Atman*. In writing it means using your most priceless gifts for exactly what they were intended—creativity.

And yet, how easy it is to get turned around. Our ego and zeal to advance can turn us outward for reinforcement in spite of our concentrated efforts to resist. It seems so simple to fix our needs with a writing class, a guru, a pill, a powder, or a drink. Sadly, too many writers fall into this trap. We can get bits and pieces of help from the outside, but nothing can align our holistic identity but ourselves.

"You make it sound so simple," writers complain. And it is simple—which makes it very difficult for some left brain thinkers. You can not put the responsibility for your holistic condition on your boss, wife, husband, friends, or associates. The control systems are yours. You must take charge. And sometimes, like the canary set free from a back-porch cage, the writer flies out, has one look at the world—and flies back into the cage. For this reason, some of us are not meant to be writers. A certain toughness is needed to be either a wild bird or a writer.

Conditioned by years of lectures about modesty, self-deprecation, and decorous behavior, it is not easy to suddenly declare the importance of I-me. It is too much like boasting; besides, there is much less risk in reaching out for some patent cure, rule book, or professional advice for what we need. But *that* energy *out there* is someone else's energy. Our own energy lies within, and in order to utilize it we must learn to trust ourselves.

These are essential terms for writing which have nothing to do with money or fame. They have to do with discipline and hard work. There is no guarantee on money and fame, but if we learn to utilize our inner resources we will have a sense of well-being that will sustain us as artists.

The Tibetan monks have a simple prayer they offer for achieving harmony:

> *My thoughts are my own thoughts*
> *My footsteps are my own footsteps*
> *My Spirit is unique among all others.*

Perhaps if we examine separately the essence of body, mind, and spirit, the meaning of holistic power will be even more clear.

Body is the most elemental of the holistic three. It is separate, though fundamentally bound to mind and spirit, and has been so since the genesis of our species. In emerging, body began as a tangible, physical identity, a vehicle from which mind and spirit followed.

A firm sense of body is vital to our creativity. Writers benefit from an awareness of body's relevance to creativity. For many people, their highest levels of achievement are reached following times of extended physical concentration. When dealing with writer's block, the obstruction might be overcome by some form of physical activity or focus.

Do not confuse this to mean you should be in top condition to write. A perfect and poignant piece of work was done a few years ago by Stewart Alsop, the *Newsweek* columnist who was dying of cancer and wrote a final column for his readers. Mr. Alsop certainly was not in Olympic condition, but he knew exactly what was happening to his body. The resultant commentary was one of the author's most eloquent moments.

Disabled writers who have little or no mobility can establish periods of serious concentration on body. Make this a forceful experience. Confront your physical presence with vigor, even if this amounts to no more than the emotional lifting of an eyelid or the emphatic pursing of the lips. Everyone's body needs a sense of validation. Regularly declare:

> *Body, I know you exist and I affirm you as an integral, important part of my creativity.*

Our burgeoning technology encourages us to abandon our physical resources for push buttons. As they do more of our work, our inherent resources are called upon to do less. That time might come when we are little disposed to do much more for our body than wash it, feed it, rest it, and find sexual satisfaction for it.

"Show me a neglected body," a therapist once said, "and I'll show you a troubled mind." How sadly true this is. When writers neglect their physical identity, their powers of production often fail. Ironically, when those so afflicted call upon a doctor it is likely he will say, "It's all in your head." Of course it's in our heads. Mind is body's closest associate.

Swami Rama, an apostle of holistic practice, said in his book, *A Practical Guide to Holistic Health:*

> *If you are in pain and there is no doctor around, everyone will tell you about some medicine or some treatment to take. You become caught up in their suggestions and fail to use common sense. One must use the mind to decide.*

The swami is saying, don't disavow the body's messages. Hear them and acknowledge them. Listen to your body. Validate it by expressing and acting on its messages.

Writers have made great progress when we realize that external energy actually is nothing more than the reflection of what exists inside us. The lure of external factors is like chasing a mirage. It can only be reached from our powers of inner energy.

A Practical Guide to Holistic Health also tells us:

When one begins to explore the inner world, we realize that the world within is larger than the one outside. One's outside world is actually very small but when the eyes are closed, we can travel to the inner place, to the sun, the moon and stars.

These are simple directions for the writer who is embarking on a course of creative anticipation. No greater Amazon twists its way through timeless jungles than exists in the rain forests of the mind. The world outside is pale in comparison. And the writer focused on this concept has access to original images and experiences greater confidence in his work.

A centered individual exudes magnetism. Such a person has almost an exultation about him that does not reflect because of outward adulation. With this power, one does not need to compromise oneself for favor, consideration, or advancement.

We must learn to listen to the wisdom of our higher self. This is the voice of our inner judgment crying for attention, one we often overrule because of fear of outside authority. This voice comes clearly, at times, when we are in some peaceful place, or have an extended period of quiet and non-interference.

Interestingly, there are writers who work in opposite conditions. I have known several for whom distraction has been such a factor in their lives that they accepted it as the norm. Having worked in the boiler-factory conditions of a newsroom and over the years having built such a tolerance for racket, it has become their form of peace. And when those reporters retire to "write that novel," they find the silence at home is deafening.

But the value of tranquility to creativity is not to be underestimated. Each of us has our own definition of the ideal writing environment. Remember the example recounted earlier about the woman who worked at home, starting after midnight when her family was asleep. She did this each night including Christmas Eve in order to finish. She had found her most ideal writing time and she was successful.

When considering our powers of right brain, which are

aligned to the holistic condition, American Plains Indians are good examples. Their surroundings were relative to their life style, form of worship, comprehension of the whole person, and the interrelation of all things. To meditate, they would withdraw into seclusion; there they would establish liaison with their inner selves and the One-Above. This state of concentration is one that all writers must envy. After all, the skyscrapers of New York City, the canals of Chicago, the tenements of Cleveland, the stockyards of Omaha are not highly inspirational. To compensate for this, writers must learn to turn inward, where the redwoods of the mind will always be available.

The Sioux were intensely aware of the relationship one must establish in order to survive as a healthy individual. The minds of the plains-dwelling Sioux were more highly tuned than was realized by the more left-brained Europeans, who presumed to judge them as savages. So predominantly right brain were the Indians, said Allen Chuck Ross, a professor at Arizona State University who studies Indian culture, that he pointed out in an article in the *Journal of American Indian Education:*

> The Indians had more appreciation for symbolic victory in war-fare. They practiced the counting of coup (touching an enemy rather than killing him) versus the more effective European desire for total annihilation.

Ross also wrote:

> The Native American view of the Supreme Being is Holistic . . . seeing whole things in overall patterns. This may be the reason why Native Americans do not have a single term to describe the Supreme Being.

In drawing these concepts into tighter focus, writers should see that the brain's participation in creative work is emphatically connected to our physical and emotional harmony. The illustrations of the American Indians should show that their intensely creative traditions and naturally holistic existence made them an important model for burnishing our own creativity.

Our minds have evolved amazingly in the past millenium, a factor that has given us dominion over all the other creatures despite their stronger teeth or fleeter legs. But as man became more technologically proficient, our cerebral hemispheres swelled and the left brain began to dominate. For advancement in technical proficiency, this has been fine. But in the process our left brain became so dominant that our creativity, or at least our means for access to it, suffered.

Now we realize that there are limitations to our left brain in spite of its dominance. We are desparately turning to the right brain, with its expansive, creative capability, and we are finding that certain basic considerations are necessary. More of a fundamental approach is needed. The left brain has prepared us for staggering equations to solve problems, but the right brain functions more simplistically and rejects the equations. It demands that we trust it.

Swami Rama explains this clearly:

We can close our eyes and have the moon and stars. All from within. The meaning is simple. We reach out and find limitations. We reach inwardly and find there are no limits. From within we may touch the far end of the Black Hole of Space, roam the Martian moons. Without, we barely escape gravity and that not for long. . . .

Reaching within is a holistic watchword. Here, the answers to most questions will be found. Business leaders often make decisions based on their instincts. One study showed they make a high percentage of correct judgments by using this instinctive system, one they implement but find it difficult to explain.

They read, listen to, and consider all angles of a problem. Then they decide solely on the basis of an inner conviction, and that conviction is often contrary to overwhelming evidence. This means that they are turned to their inner resources in spite of the swell of external opinions. Writers would do well to develop this resource.

A certain creative assessment plays a vital role in making decisions. A hunch will overwhelm an abundance of research. In war, science, space, or medicine, there have been instances when an individual making a critical decision relied on an inner directive that proved to be correct.

For those of us who work under stress for long periods and then come home and try to write, we must remember that our systems need a time of transition. Many writers are in too great a hurry to begin. You must realize that it is important to get in touch with your whole being *before* confronting the creative process. One exercise that works well is a simple walk around the block.

Another effective means of preparing the mind is a breathing exercise in which you simply force out the stomach, thus drawing down the diaphragm. This fills the lungs from the lower portion up, instead of filling them from the top down, as in rib-cage breathing. When the breath is drawn in from the belly up, exhale without pause. Feel out this rhythm; practice the in-and-out breaths with no hesitation between. As you do, the benefits will be felt immediately in the stomach walls, which traditionally are held in tightly, due to our social distaste for a potbelly. To right brain thinkers a potbelly is no factor.

During this exercise, feel the freshly aerated blood in the system and feel how the liberated stomach walls, no longer painfully sucked in, add to the sense of relief. The mind is now calmer; breathing correctly will have relaxed it.

The next move is to lower your shoulders from their hunched-up position. Lowered, the shoulders allow you to write more freely. Shoulders and stomach relaxed, body and mind allow greater access to the right brain.

With the change in brain command, hundreds of alert systems throughout the body and mind are quieting. A consciousness of time is lessened. A greater sense of harmony takes over. A level of right brain creativity can now be established.

It is important to remember that human curiosity will always take some of us into the twilight zones of bad judgment. But by using common sense, you may safely channel your creative energy into your writing by establishing a holistic balance. No trance, astral traveling, or out-of-body experience is necessary to write. And certainly drugs or alcohol do not enhance the process. The rigors of these extremes are more damaging than the results are purposeful.

An additional factor for many writers is that it is not possible for them to drop out for long periods of solitary introspection. Right brain perceivers are also left brain providers; as such, they have homes, families, cats, and obligations. Therefore we must learn to settle for some portion of the day, every day, to express our creative force.

Another exercise for relieving mental pressures is to find a comfortable upright position, not one lying down. If physically disabled, lie flat if necessary, but think upright. Allow a bit of time for the breathing exercise, then rest a few moments before starting:

> *Concentrate on some distant speck by closing your eyes and focusing on the inside of your lids. Count and (mentally) touch each toe of the right foot with the right hand. Begin with the little toe, continuing to the next and the next. Speak the name of each toe as you count. Now move to the foot and (mentally) hold it and declare its identity. In your mind hold it tightly. Next the ankle, and on up the torso. Continue to the head, each time calling the parts by name.*

It has been asked, "What do I do if somebody comes in while I'm talking to my toes?" The answer is simple. You merely say, "Oh, it's nothing really. I'm merely having a little talk with my body so that it and my mind will become better aligned." After this, you may anticipate a hasty exit by the visitor.

Remember that stomach muscles are very important. The stomach is always victimized by stress. Take the time to concentrate on relaxing those muscles. The buttocks are also stress victims. As the largest area of muscle mass in our body, they instinctively bunch up during tension.

The exercises have worked for many writers because the full concentration of mind's powers screen out distractions. An exchange of energy between body and mind takes place, and the resulting strength gives us a sense of well-being that makes writing easier.

A healthy spirit is a celebration of body and mind, a barometer of our general state. For writers, there is no greater asset than being of good spirit. The spirit appears at the moment of birth and is last to depart in death. Persons who have experienced out-of-body adventures say that spirit leaves on a journey of its own after death, but can return in another life.

What does this mean to writers? If there exists some connection with the mystical, other lives, and some element of a Supreme Being, it can only be understood through spirit. Here is the purest essence of our identity.

Writers hold impressive influential powers, and we are accountable for how we use these powers. Coupled to writing, spiritual energy can be misused due to the temptations of life.

As you grow and develop command of your craft, you will come to realize the full force of ego. Since you are all blessed/cursed with ego, it must be channeled properly. We have all heard about writers who achieved early success, instant money, and lost everything when their egos slammed out of control.

Spirit is the natural governor for ego. If you wonder about a decision, do not ask your ego for the answer, consult your higher power, which is always associated with better purpose.

As the reflection of mind and body, spirit is our avenue for the most effective means of communication. We meditate through spirit. For this reason writers should stay in touch with what makes them feel satisfied with themselves. The Eastern philosophers say that to do good is to feel good about it.

To avoid confusion, understand that a state of holistic harmony does not mean that we are immune to life's trials, but it does help us to endure adversity. Spiritual peace is every writer's greatest reward. No wealth can compensate us as well as the experience of having contributed to our society. High purpose is the act of providing the greatest benefit and the least harm possible. No writer should write to intentionally hurt someone else. There will be times when the truth will be harmful to another, but this is different from the deliberate desire to do damage. Budd Schulberg, one of our finest contemporary authors, once said, "You scratch an honest writer and you'll find a moralist."

Material success in writing is not always possible. Spiritual success in our craft is always possible. After all, the finest artists are not always the ones before the public's eye. There will always be an element of timeliness in material success which may not fall in your favor.

For every Rodin, Faulkner, or Mozart, there probably were others who were equally gifted, not widely known. Their time was not right.

Realize that in each lifetime there is only space for so many discoveries, so many material successes. And although some will disagree and protest the waste, we must understand that in the broader view (right brain) there is no such thing as waste. Waters that spill over a dam into the sand are not wasted. Those same molecules have been recirculating about the plant for eons and will recirculate again in their own good time.

Someone once said that the reward of turning the wheel is turning the wheel. Wheat is quickly eaten and then forgotten. But the memory of those who harvested the wheat fields lives long after the chaff has been scattered. Taking this view is spiritual; it is patient; it leads to peace of mind.

But what about those times when my spirit is low, asked a young writer? And it is admitted, there will be many times when our spirits are at rock bottom. But we must understand that this happens when we reach for *exterior energy* and *status* to such an extent that we neglect our holistic harmony.

Fortunately, with holistic knowledge, we can deal with low spirits by *returning to basics*. Writers must never forget this, so great are the ups and downs and broken hearts in this profession. Returning to basics is something akin to rebirth, but each time we do we are smarter, since we have the advantage of having survived our previous mistakes.

Reestablish contact with body, then with mind. Renew your contact through exercises and meditation. And as you do your sense of well-being, of spiritual energy, will be renewed, reflecting the centered harmony of your total being.

Review

Each writer has strengths and weaknesses. For this reason, underline those passages in this chapter that most directly apply to you.

Remember, the essence of holistic understanding is to constantly seek to achieve the *greatest simplicity*. Avoid complication and convolution whenever possible.

Exercise

The purpose of a guidebook is to provide a more personal example. To that end, this exercise is intended as a homework assignment:

> *Using some provision in this chapter that made an impression on you, write who, what, when, where, why, and how that impression applies to you. Be honest with your feelings and create a story that relates to this particular instance.*

Suggested Reading

The Autobiography of a Yogi, by Paramhansa Yogananda. The Self-Realization Fellowship, 3880 San Rafael Ave., Los Angeles, Calif. 90065 (1952).

Communications Vibrations, by Larry L. Barker. (page 133—"How Successful Men Make Decisions") Prentice-Hall, Inc., Englewood Cliffs, N.J. (1974).

The Snow Leopard, by Peter Matthiessen. The Viking Press, 625 Madison Avenue, New York, N. Y. (1978).

Black Elk Speaks, by John G. Neihardt. Pocket Books, 630 Fifth Ave., New York, N. Y. 10020 (1977).

Psychodietetics, by Dr. E. Cheraskin and Dr. W. M. Ringsdorf, Jr., with Arline Brecher, Bantam Book, 666 Fifth Ave., New York, N.Y. 10020 (1974).

WRITING ASSIGNMENTS

Writing assignments are designed to sharpen specific areas of your writing. They are best done as little stories that have a beginning, middle, and end.

Start with the first assignment of this chapter and work through them to the last one. Time is not important.

Each subject has a few suggestions or directions that might help the writer who is struggling for an inspiration. Whether you steam off in your own directions or rely somewhat on the written provisions, make a commitment to go where your energy takes you. The assignments in this chapter have been tested in classroom conditions and they do work—sometimes miracles.

Before you begin an assignment, allow the possibilities to filter through your mind and activate your imagination. Jot down any ideas you get; rely as little as possible on your memory.

The story you will write must have background, plot, and characterization. The background is a stage on which your story (plot) and people (characterizations) will play. Allow yourself to become each of these people, the places they appear, and the story they act out. As the writer, you become all things—you are creator.

Notice too how the mix of people, story, and location begins to develop an energy of its own as you write. In a sense, your inner resources have actually breathed life and believability into the story.

Each assignment should be about two pages in length, but do not worry about length until you have finished your idea. Compacting your assignment into two pages comes with editing, which should be farthest from your mind as you write.

Once you begin editing, replace any weak words with stronger ones; deleting any superfluous paragraphs or move them to more strategic places in the story. This gives you wonderful practice. The need to write in two pages when your story begs for five is the dilemma professionals live with every day.

Your assignments, in reality, are little novels, sparse but complete, containing all the fundamental elements of a larger piece. They have beginning, middle, and end. They have characterization, plot, and location or background.

The beginning is our first consideration. It is probably the most important part of the story. The beginning has to command the reader's attention, actually reach out and take that reader by the lapels. Additionally, the beginning has to serve the right mix of characterization, background, and story or plot. The chemistry of that mix depends on the story and the writer's judgment and experience. If you make mistakes in this area, good. That's how you learn and eventually realize, "Now I can see that less background and more of Emily's character would have made a much stronger beginning." The need for chemistry now makes sense.

This is why writing instructors continue to insist that you cannot teach someone to write. You inspire them and provide technique and guidelines, but they learn by doing. Writing the assignments is an excellent way to learn.

It is also important to establish that the beginning of any story is where the writer provides the rules for the reader. Reading and writing comprise a game; the writer is in control. Therefore the reader cannot play the game unless the rules are provided as early as possible. A few of the rules for the beginning are: (1) Identify the characters who appear. (2) Provide some time frame and background; let the reader know there is a story taking place and that the people, places, and things are going somewhere. Most readers dislike a stagnant story that gives no sense of movement. Whenever possible, without giving away too much, allow the reader to have an idea what is going on. The reader is eager to play, but must be included in the game. The name of the game is *please read this story.*

The middle of the story, generally, is where questions are intensified, characters show some growth or development or direction, and backgrounds are more familiar. The chemistry of the story, its writing style and message, should be established by this time. The reader should be comfortably informed about what is going on or what the writer wants him to believe is going on. Momentum is building; expectations are developing as the plot increases its tempo. This middle is the writer's territory. Less concern for losing the reader is felt and more impetus of right brain projections take place. The writer's creativity is at full pendulum here. And again, this middle must be pregnant with questions.

The ending requires a little more regulation. Any number of issues must be resolved in one way or another. The dilemma, characterizations, and story are narrowed to a more controllable size. Less of the wild middle stirring is possible. By now the reader is on the edge of the chair awaiting answers or at least indications. For most writers the ending is where they adhere to good housekeeping and start to clean up the mess they made in the middle. Ideally, the story will be tied up in a neat bowknot. But remember, the word is *usually*, because stories are highly unique and no rigid set of definitions will work for all. If a rule were given that could stand the writing test, it would be "Be flexible."

When the assignment is done, read it, pencil-edit any errors or changes, and test all persons, places, and things with the five W's. Let there be smells, textures, tastes, and sounds as well as sights.

Now is also the time to deal with the length of your assignment. If it is too long, take a narrower view of the subject. "A Day in June" might have to become "An Hour in June." When the needed refinement is worked, it is time to consider the first-page impact of your story. Does your first line grab that reader? Is there a chemistry of characterization, background, and story to lead the reader into the subsequent pages? And remember, no effective first page is possible until the whole story is done. After the editing process, the first page you began with might be lined out by now. This is why a writer is never certain of that first page until the story is written.

Now begins a critical stage that writers have named the "wasteland" or "tundra" of the craft. Rewriting, again and again, is that wasteland. Refinement of creative work tries the most durable and motivated of us, tries us sometimes to our limits. This is where the aspirants and the achievers are established. The bones of fine talent dot this tundra, but such are the demands of the craft. The beauty of that first thought that came to mind and then found its way onto paper must now be honed and polished.

And this is the beauty of writing assignments. They are the proving grounds. Their limited size allows you to develop in a manageable, more visible space. It is foolish to whip off a few pages and then whisk them off to a publisher to get a rejection slip. Though considered badges of honor and dedication, rejection slips don't teach you anything or show you where you erred. It's like trying out a homemade parachute that's never been tested by jumping out of an airplane—a more reasonable proving ground is needed.

So, what about those of you biting your nails because an inspiration has not come from your first assignment? Do not despair. Your mind merely needs a bit of priming, a push to get it started. So write your feelings about not having anything to write about. Use the subject as a start and say why it won't work for you. Be critical; express the extent of your feelings. If you are frustrated, say so; go into detail. And remember this—some excellent ideas come from subjects that are not related to your inspiration. When this happens, go with your inspiration.

A mysterious energy takes place when writing. The brain shifts to right mode and images form. The writer agonizing over the lack of an idea suddenly finds that several ideas have appeared. Writing seems to initiate the mechanism.

One more task remains after you have written, edited, rewritten, and perhaps revised your first page. This is a delayed performance called seasoning. Put your assignment on the shelf and let it season until the next day.

Okay, now it's tomorrow. Take your assignment off the shelf and read through your pages. In only twenty-four hours you will have found that parts of it have been forgotten. In a way, it's as though some stranger wrote parts of it, and this is a blessing. In order to read your own work critically, it has to have some aspect of unfamiliarity. If the pages are memorized, they are almost impossible to evaluate. The critic needs to have a fresh mind.

What you are doing is exchanging the writer side of your mind for the reader's side. To do this you must put aside all forgiveness ("I know what I meant, I just didn't say it") and isolate your errors with the cold detachment of a stranger. You must read as though you paid for this story and now you want your money's worth.

If any part lacks clarity, use marginal notes for the writer's guidance when it is time to fix it. If there is something you find that is very good, mark this too. Writers love to find approval as well. Demand that backgrounds, personalities, and the story be believable. The details must be convincing.

Take these assignments seriously. They are the proving grounds from which your most impressive novels, short stories, and articles might be born. They will become impressive additions to your idea file. And it's a good idea to file them with their marginal notations for your later appraisal. Writers develop quite rapidly, and the writing, along with your observations, will be assets at a later time. In addition to development of ideas, the assignments will tell you—at some distant time—how far you have come.

One of My Favorite Things. Relax and think about this topic. Allow some of your favorite things to parade through your mind. Many of them have a favorite story attached. From these images, form a simple plot; jot down your plans, don't trust your memory.

The idea can be fiction or otherwise, as long as you make it happen in your mind and then on the pages.

A Period in History I Would Like to Share. Again, sort through your mind and history to find those times that are important to you. Let yourself become a Walter Mitty, the man who lived in his imagination. If it helps, take liberties with history, or make notes and do a bit of research. Create accurate dialogue. After all, Paul Revere did not say, "Let's hit it, fellows, the limeys are coming."

A Bad Moment. Writers facing a writing assignment complain if it deals with negative subjects. Again, this is an impediment you must overcome. Writers have no immunity to the pain or stress of life. In many ways we intensify it with the constant search for reality. Ironically, some of the best writing assignments done have been the ones dealing with pain or tragedy. This is why experienced writers urge us to confront our pain and distress. Sometimes it is more clearly etched into our consciousness than happiness.

First Love. This subject can be autobiographical or imaginary. Well-defined characters are essential, and good dialogue will also be important. Daring and imagination can originate some surprising directions. Explore them.

Fear. Dealing with such a basic emotion will often take you back to your childhood for the clearest definition. Love, hatred, anxiety, hunger—all are related to life and thus are fundamental to writing. Draw on your experiences with fear. Think fear, touch it, taste it, and smell it. What does it look like, sound like? Search for these answers, then build the story.

Good-Bye. Capturing this simplest of experiences is a great workshop exercise. "Good-bye" is a simple if broad possibility for a story. The term is so common in life and in writing. Is its meaning somehow lost in its familiarity? Find out. Sort through your good-byes and weave a story about one of them.

Falling in Love. Stories on this subject outnumber the falling leaves, yet there is always room for fascinating additions. The subject should reflect the individuality of the writer. Most of all, use daring and imagination.

Daisy. Flower or fauna? Think about Daisy and give the name careful consideration. There is a feel to this name. For almost all of us, the mention of it conjures up the image of—something. For this reason, "Daisy" might almost write itself. Starting is the slowest part, but once moving, let your right brain take off—even if it leads you into outrageous territory.

Boris—A Profile. In writing a profile, you are expected to give the reader an intimate look at a character. Profile is exactly what it implies: the outline that best describes the entity within those lines. With this in mind, ask yourself, What is a Boris? Search for a clear, descriptive view of Boris. Perhaps a glimpse into his mind or behaviorisms will provide this depth. Does your character act like a Boris? Does he fulfill those expectations the name suggests? We want Boris on a pin like a moth, and we want him thus within the two-page story you write.

You Are in Love with a Unicorn. For some writers a little bit of research will be in order. For others, the less they know from other sources the better they will work. This writer prefers to work solely on the spontaneous images that come with the mere mention of *unicorn*. Daring and adventuresomeness might be the direction to take. Or you might find more inspiration in some philosophical avenue. By exploring, you will learn, and in learning discover a potential far greater than you imagined.

My Shame. Whether truth or illusion, success with this topic will depend on the personal emphasis you invest in it. The shame need not be yours, but it should be something you were close enough to, at this painful moment, to focus into. The shame of some public figure might have been close enough to stimulate your vicarious responses. Explore the terms of this shame and the consequences it brings. The story will come, but first you must experience in real feelings the subject you will write.

Sylvia Chimerinski—A Profile. Envision the name in order to focus on Sylvia as someone you have known. Her name gives you a lot of help; from there her identity should come easier. Find her eyes and face; give her proportions. Let her grow as your right brain expands her form and etches her features. As Sylvia comes alive, she will take part in her own creation. You will see her mannerisms and personality emerge. As all this happens, you will see first hand how writers have to come to sword's point with their characters. And in the process of creating Sylvia, have a talk with her. Learn her feelings and opinions. Writers do have real talks with their characters, which adds enormously to the pleasure of writing.

Dead Horse Flats, New Mexico. First of all, there is no such place in New Mexico, but a look at the map might help focus on what, where, and when such a settlement might have or could have been. A community is no better or worse than the people living there. This, along with its background, will be important to consider. Again, you will experience the magnificent power of creation as life and surroundings take form and bits of history fit together. Once more, your powers of right brain will serve you.

Tina Grows Up. This subject will bring a predictable response to many of you: a little girl growing up. This is fine, but you should consider a few of the alternatives as they sift into your thinking. What would be a *different* approach? This is the professional's challenge from a market that has seen just about all the angles there are. There are always others. They come from writers who refuse to accept the traditional answers. Give this some thought before you begin.

The Tracks on the Moon Lead to . . . The daring writer will have time with this assignment. But the topic is not one for science fiction writers alone. One of the demands for this assignment is for the writer to believe wholly in the subject matter compiled. An editor or experienced reader can always tell when the writer is actively involved with a piece of work and when it is done at arm's length. *Conviction* might be the watchword for this assignment. Believe and it will not only serve you, it will amaze you.

Surprise. In fairness to your right brain, no suggestions or comments will be offered with this assignment. The most helpful statement, without interfering with your thinking, is to give full consideration to the power of the word. Its energy is—surprising.

My First Kiss. Aim your thinking beyond the initial triteness of the subject. The powers of imagination and the daring to explore beyond the accepted expectations of this topic must be considered. In telling a story, the position from which it is told has a lot to do with the effectiveness of that story. Overall, writing is learning, and this assignment should be a good example of that fact.

The Sun Will Set in the Morning. The impression some writers will get from this topic is that it comes from some quotation or saying. It does not, although that should not be a factor in putting together this story. The subject is a springboard into the story. Where it will take us is something the writer knows least of all.

The One You Love Plans to Kill You . . . but Doesn't Know that You Know. An interesting situation can emerge from this assignment. Great dialogue is also possible. The dramatic potential here comes from the fact that one person has information the other does not have. The fact that a life might be in jeopardy heightens the stakes. Yet in order to use the information most effectively, the first person must not reveal what he knows. Herein lies the excitement as the game speeds up. The reader will wonder how the person in the stronger position will use this information. Most of all, the assignment will challenge your ability to confine the action to two pages.

This Assignment has No Name, but Its First Line Must Be: The Door Stood Ajar. This is a good exercise in storytelling. The first line of the assignment must begin with the title. In some minds this will pave the way to a conclusion. For others it will be an impediment. Your command of storytelling should be tested in this assignment.

Is That You, David? Is That You, Sonia? Two characters come to mind with little delay. But what is going on? Who are they and what are they doing, our interrogator wonders? And the right brain takes over here, filling in the spaces with creative explanations.

The First Thing You See in the Morning Is Your Assignment. The best way to prepare for this subject is to give it some thought at bedtime. Prepare or precondition your mind to focus on the first item your eyes find upon awakening. In some instances it might be your blanket seam. If so, that's your assignment. The purpose of this and the other exercises is to challenge your powers of creativity and perception and better prepare you for the writing ahead.

Eavesdrop on a Conversation and Then Use That Information to Write a Story. Writers must learn to become intensive listeners. It is important to hear how others talk in order to bring that same realness to the writing. Listening to what is said and then taking those few fragments of conversation to the typewriter is the stuff of convincing stories. Use those real words in the story you weave. Observe and, most of all, understand the effect they have on the story.

You Have Finished a Novel—Now Write the Last Page. A little imagination is needed here. First you have to imagine the novel, then work it through your mind to some sort of conclusion. This done, write the last two pages, which will reveal how well you developed this nonexistent novel in the first place. In doing so, a better grasp of how a story is constructed comes to light. You see that a story is nothing more than a collection of pieces that are connected with words.

A Quiet Presence Waits at Your Door—It Is Death. If you feel a little uncomfortable at first, such is not unusual for this assignment. Still, give this some thought. The writer (you) and not death is in charge of this assignment. In some ways the writer has the advantage. Explore the ways you can use that advantage.

As one final exercise, think of an expensive book you might pay a lot of money for and then ask yourself what this book must contain to be worth so much. Write down these considerations. In addition to your own, a few of them might be:

clarity	readable
excitement	comprehensible
new information	believable
sharp characterizations	helpful
good dialogue	touching
worthy statement	revealing
good research	interesting
commendable	lasting

Use this list, along with any additions you feel are in order, and apply the qualities above to your own writing. Some of your assignments will have a higher scoring than others. A simple way to score is to count the qualities you find and subtract them from the lines listed above. If you find twelve out of the sixteen on the list, you are above average. But the scoring is not as important as the comparisons you find with other assignments. The one with only six of the sixteen obviously needs some work. Mark the qualities that are lacking and then consider improving on this need. It can tell you a lot about your writing if one or more items are consistently missing in most of your assignments.

These writing exercises never fail to provoke a good deal of self-discovery. Writers desperately need to know about themselves. That is why it is essential to do all the assignments.

The brain holds a wealth of material from life and lessons learned. This resource becomes an energy that emerges as creative expression. Some of the least likely topics will inspire amazresults. Our creative chemistry works that way.

Writers routinely admit, "I never know what's coming out of my head." The right brain makes us very aware of this and therefore demands that we trust it.

The intent of the assignments is to generate ideas. When this happens, write them down for your files. If they are lively ideas, give them priority.

Writers with various stages of block must know that the assignments are the best medicine to take for their creative ills. The assignments generate the needed antibodies to combat writer's block. All assignments have been tested in a classroom; they do work. Trust them and learn about yourself.

RESEARCH

One of the common problems that plague new writers is that they begin working before they do their homework—the research. This causes them to run dry, and they end up blocked because they are out of information. The left brain will then suggest they are stupid and should find something more practical to do, like mushroom farming.

Proper research prepares the writer for the larger work ahead and prevents the lapses caused by scant information. The writer must first become an authority on a subject, and research is the only way to do it.

A good idea must have power, enough to move a story from opening page to conclusion, but an idea is only one of the ingredients in a well-constructed book. Effective writing must have a foundation of good research. Writing makes your story readable, but research makes it believable.

Let's take the example of James Michener, a writer with a background as a history teacher. His books are many; each is a monument to extensive research, a depth of information that inspires intricate plots, interesting characterizations, and overwhelming background detail. Some Michener readers warn: Don't begin a Michener book—you'll have to finish it. Those who don't take this advice end up hooked.

An aspiring writer once asked where to find the best sources for research. "Everywhere" is about the only reasonable reply. Your own life is number one. Then come libraries, tax records, old letters, and newspaper clippings. In barbershops you can listen to the natives speak the local language. You can study the local rituals in saloons, in churches, and at courthouse trials; you can observe mating dances at the local disco—all is research. The "where" depends on what you are writing about.

The experienced writer knows that it's important to keep both eyes and ears open. Suppress the desire to talk. You already know what you have to say. If you listen, you can learn what someone else has to say. Research is information; don't discount old wives' tales, legends, folklore, gossip, and hearsay. Even when you can't use this category of information, you will find a trend or an indication that might lead you to further sources.

Like gossips, writers must learn to be professional listeners. Tune in on the affairs of others. Wars have been fought, won and lost on the strength or lack of one side's listening ability.

Research is also hard, plodding, fascinating work. You might sort through reams of paper before finding one nugget of information. The process might take longer than the actual writing of the book. Still, research is essential. It provides the details and minutiae which transform the reading of a story into experiencing the story.

Writing fills out the center of a story, but research fills out the corners; it gives you the type of stone in the fireplace, background on the neighborhood where "she" runs the beauty shop, the mechanical condition of "her" car, along with its appearance. This deeply involves your reader's imagination because the brain builds images from fragments of detail.

Some writers find research more interesting than the eventual writing. They become paid researchers, and other writers rely on them for details they would rather not dig out themselves.

An example of interesting research is the work that went into the biography of Tom Bass, a Missouri horseman born in slavery. There was no information on Tom Bass in most public libraries. Newspaper clippings were filed at the local paper, but the most important background material came from nineteenth century records found in the attic storage space of the Boone County, Missouri, courthouse in Columbia. This county seat courthouse had priceless information about such things as Daniel Boone, the Kentucky Indian fighter, spending time in the area prior to the Louisiana Purchase.

Ledgers were stacked floor to ceiling in this dusty, cobweb-draped attic. The information was so concentrated you could almost smell it. Records were written in the laborious long-hand of the time, since typewriters had not been invented. One could imagine those quill pens dipped into brown India ink. One ledger had records of householder levies. One family was taxed for: "Two cows, four head of horses, 21 chickens and four ducks; Toby, a male negro slave of good working age but dangerous when drinking." The implication was that Toby's drinking might have some reflection on his taxability.

Newspapers thrive on public records, but many writers don't realize this is a prime source of information. Exploring tax records can turn up material you didn't imagine existed. These records are public information, free and accessible.

Newspapers themselves are another good source, but the average writers researching a book will rarely find newspaper librarians inclined to help them. It adds to their workload to "help out" an outside writer. A little front-office prodding can work wonders if the writer has such a contact.

Public libraries are also a source of newspaper information. Librarians collect papers for their records and offer them for public use. So, if the newspaper won't share their clipping file, the library will.

During the initial periods of research the writer is least selective about material. Gather a bit of everything. Later, the material can be gleaned for more specific information. You often end up with more material than will ever be used, but that is fine, too. A famous author has said that the writer with too much research gives the impression that no greater authority on this subject can be found. Additionally, this confidence comes through the writing and enhances your credibility.

Detailed studies of cities, towns, and villages are critical to a story's believability. Readers who have been to these places, or have read about them, must feel that what they are reading is authentic. Beyond living there, no greater means for creating this familiarity is possible without extensive research. Especially desirable are those tidbits of esoteric note which delight the discerning reader. The fact that New York was purchased for about twenty-six dollars' worth of trade goods has intrigued readers for three hundred years.

Conversation is always helpful in gaining information. The clever listener will be careful to only add a, "Yes, of course," or an occasional "Do tell" in order not to cut off the speaker. The art of listening is the art of keeping your mouth clamped shut in spite of your desire to be the expert.

For the writer to listen effectively it is helpful to have an understanding of a basic human need: our innate desire to be heard. This need to talk is termed *discharge*. So strong is this desire that even an experienced interviewer will sometimes break into a conversation to establish a few keen points. When this happens, you interrupt your speaker's continuity and often end the conversation.

In the process of capturing accents, colloquialisms, and ethnic phrasing, the writer must hear or read about the local vernacular. For example, in a formal *interview* a Texan might talk a lot less Texas than he would in a *conversation* with another person.

The new writer should make a practice of listening in on conversations without making himself too obvious. Sit near an animated exchange. Show no outward interest, but listen intently. Though it appears a little hammy, take a newspaper and pretend to read. This is an old prop, but it works. The newspaper all but shouts that you are not interested it anything but the news.

Take along a pad and jot down notable expressions you have heard. Make a note of accents that indicate some distant influence. Note the rhythm of speech. Convincing prose captures this, and the way to accomplish the right note in your writing is to practice the dialogue with your typewriter.

A writer listening in on a conversation between two older men said that when one urged the other to lean over and take a good look at his appendectomy scar, the listener all but had to clench his fists to keep from interrupting.

"I wanted to tell them that the scar they were looking at was nothing, that if they wanted to see a *real* scar, they should take a peek at mine," the interviewer confessed.

Will and Ariel Durant were that rare blend of talent, the writer and the researcher. It was difficult to tell where one's talent ended and the other's began. This literary (and love) match was made in paradise. All writers should be so lucky as to be married to their researcher.

After a long period in the lonely role of writing, there are those who thoroughly enjoy their research. It's grand to prowl the libraries and bookstores, freed from the confines of "the room." Even when we see our colleagues in a local bar, we know they are "researching," too.

Research allows a fictitious character to rise from the pages in lifelike form. Each added dimension of this character's personality lends animation. Soon our character has an identity, with strong likes and dislikes. In researching characters for a novel, it is common to develop the personalities to accommodate the plot. When it is not logical that Mildred will change her mind about John's quirk, the writer merely remodels Mildred's thinking to help the story.

But in nonfiction we have a different situation. As with so many biographies, the writer has a story idea laid out, but the research of the character begins to dispute the story line. In nonfiction we can't change the character and disavow the facts—that's unprofessional. So we change the story to accommodate the information. In other words, nonfiction characters do control their story, while in fiction it's the other way around.

Writers collecting research for their projects will sometimes find gaps in their information. Certain segments of history will be sketchily recounted while others are recorded in depth. Some writers state clearly that little detail exists to presume one direction or another. This said, they proceed to presume.

Interviewing is an art both fiction and nonfiction writers should master. The skill of effective interviewing is a profession in itself. Again, the writer must know when to talk and when to shut up. Be sure to do your homework on the subject. Attempting to interview someone without knowing anything about them is foolhardy in itself. Another rule is to ask the easy questions first. This way, if a person becomes offended by some personal or sensitive question, the interview is not ruined.

Interviewing should come off as a conversation, not a grilling. Exchange a few banalities just to warm up, although you both know it's more of an interrogation. The ability to prepare with a more right-brained approach is to the writer's advantage. Questions that are imaginative or different cause the subject to think and not rely on the same old answers that were used the month before. Interviews all tend to run together and the subjects often find them boring.

Once, to change the tone of a desperately dull interview with Los Angeles Mayor Tom Bradley, the interviewer asked, "Mayor Bradley, what type of shorts do you wear—boxer or jockey?"

The mayor never blinked as he replied, "Boxer." He was unquestionably cool under fire. But the reporter had his attention.

An example given to illustrate the perils of interviewing a personality without first preparing is shown in the story about the reporter who interviewed the great blues singer, B. B. King. The interview was insightful, the reporter thought. But the next day, he discovered that the story King told was almost a word-for-word duplicate of the jacket blurb on King's latest album. Luckily, the people who read albums didn't read the news interview.

A similarity exists between police work and good interviewing. Both do a lot of what-iffing, although the interviewer must be more diplomatic.

Writers must realize that research is not much of a right brain task. The process is somewhat systematic, with lists to follow and precise information to be gathered; rules, guides, and directions are the name of this game. Research is primarily left brain work, although the right brain can give us intuitive hunches to explore.

Use the shortcuts to book research by poring over the table of contents, index, introduction, preface, and bibliography of the book. All are useful ways to save time and avoid reading things that are not relative to your idea. Look for the buzzwords in an index that might refer to your subject.

In using this system your reading becomes more selective. Yet there often seems to be about twice the material you needed. Remember that knowing more than you can use in your book lends authenticity to your work.

Another helpful idea is to study the structure of a book similar to the one you want to write. The experienced writer will study a succesful book to see how it is organized. Every published book is a guide of sorts.

Writers with ambitions to write for magazines must learn the content of the magazine first. Learn its format, style, and structure. Book publishing is somewhat more flexible, but writers must know something about the expectations of the publication they hope to impress. Writing teachers love to use the example of *Popular Mechanics* magazine receiving poetry because some writer did not go to the trouble to read the magazine.

As far as writing a book, no one merely sits down to create. When the author begins typing, much of the hard work is done. The project that began as an idea has been expanded into a story line, then into a plot. The characters have been drawn out in biographical form. Places and things in the story have been explored and written out. Overall, the research for the project will have taken a fair amount of time before you begin to write.

After a period of research, the writer will know a good deal about the subject. You already know much of the information you gather at this point. It's almost time to conclude the research and prepare for its assimilation into the story. The temptation to search longer keeps the writer away from the original object: writing the book. Some writers stall this way to avoid the lonely days ahead. Avoid this trap.

By the time the writer is ready to begin, there are notes, outlines, profiles, characterizations, background information, and sometimes maps and pictures surrounding him or her. The research has been like auditioning musicians. Now the writer must direct them in harmony.

It is much the same as with a symphony director: The writer must listen to the research as it blends into the story. There will be times when it is lovely to hear, and other times when it is discordant. At these times, stop and find out what is going on. Your mind is telling you something. Most of the time, though, the material will sing. You have done your research well and the chances are good that it will pay off.

A California writer once said that to him good stories are like good chocolate chip cookies. The ones made with the fewest chips are not very tasty compared to the fat ones.

"These are busy cookies," he says. "I love a busy cookie." And readers love busy books as well, if the enormous advances this author commands are any indication.

For many of us, a certain seductiveness exists in research. The very qualities that make you a writer make you vulnerable to the parade of assorted subject matter you will find. The encyclopedia, for instance, can lead you far astray from your original direction. Open the pages to Dublin. There on the opposite page is Julian Dubuque, the first landowner in Spanish Louisiana. He was buried with the honors of a chief by the Fox Indians. A city was named for him. Great, but what does it have to do with Dublin, the original subject?

During the research phase the writer will find ideas that have potential for interesting stories to come. Write them down for your idea file. Any one of them could be your next book.

One of the best friends a writer can have is the librarian.

Libraries are highly sophisticated storage systems whose inner workings defy anyone who doesn't have a degree in library science. You need a degree just to ask for some information in the library. Therefore, library research would be impossible without the librarian. A national "Love your Librarian Day" would be very much in order, for they have unquestionably contributed to more volumes with less recognition than any other services.

In this chapter the emphasis has been put on the importance of doing research before beginning to write. New writers are puzzled when told that the hard work is all done when a writer sits down to write. James Michener told the Santa Barbara Writers Conference that it is not unusual for him to spend two or three years researching a book that took him less than a year to write.

Michener is a good example of the writer who stops to listen to his research, asking and testing it to make sure he is following his guidelines. Sometimes the sheer volume of research will change the original direction of the work, but the writer must always be in charge.

Exercise

Take a name, any name, then slowly build an identity about it. Give this name everything possible to make it a real character. Likes, dislikes, interests, and the lack of them are important. Write as many pages as necessary to create a living person.

When this is done, make a list of things this character likes to do, places the character enjoys going. List them in detail; include cars, friends, hobbies, and talents.

By now you have created someone who is familiar. You understand his fears, concerns, loves, and so on. There is a good chance you have a certain fondness for your character. Too bad—now you must kill him off.

Write two pages about the death of this character. The more believable you have made him, the more difficult it will be to eliminate him.

Writers often feel a deep sense of loss when such an assignment is completed. The purpose is to show how much personal energy goes into effective writing when your research has a certain depth.

WRITERS DISCUSS
THE BLOCK

Right brain creativity and its nemesis, writer's block, are as topical for well-known authors as for beginners. In this chapter some of the best-known writers verbalize their feelings on how they deal with writer's block. Several speak out on the state of the art in general. And even those who declined had interesting responses:

Irving Stone and his wife were out of the country on an extended research trip for his next book.

Judith Krantz and her husband were in Paris, where she was preparing her novel *Mistral's Daughter* for television. Max Perkins once said in reference to F. Scott Fitzgerald's need to work in France: "The better their work the farther from home they seem to go."

If this is true, then Alex Haley, working at the time in Morocco, must have had another *Roots* in the making.

For *Joan Didion* and her husband, *John Gregory Dunne*, to discuss writer's block at mid-stage of the new books they were writing would have been something akin to a curse, she confided: ". . . too fearful to talk about the process out loud."

Eudora Welty, nestled in her Jackson, Mississippi, home, said, "I am not able to help you in right brain creativity discussions. I don't know a thing about it. I am sorry."

This is ironic, because Miss Welty's work is about as right brain and creative as any in print and has been a pattern for writers in America and around the world.

George Plimpton, editor of *The Paris Review*, was too busy interviewing Norman Mailer for *People* magazine to make a statement on writer's block. However, he did enclose a small subscription form offering twelve issues of his magazine for $48, and made the additional offer to become a *The Paris Review* associate for $1,000.

Alistair Cooke, obviously immune to writer's block, said: "I'm sorry—I myself have never had writer's block. I learned early on that being a writer is like being a plumber. You work every day at the same time; write when you don't feel like it. Imagine a plumber who couldn't turn off a raging faucet because he had plumber's block."

Those writers who did contribute to this chapter speak out on how to overcome the problems; in some cases they address as well the issue of holistic power and the spirutal forces that can develop in writing. As they do, you find vivid examples from the preceding chapters and the lessons that are supported by these words.

Ted Berkman is a Santa Barbara writer with New York roots. He was critically applauded for the biography *To Seize the Passing Dream,* which captured the life and times of James Whistler. Berkman has also written many other books and screenplays. Recently he returned to public attention when Ronald Reagan was elected President of the United States. Among Reagan's screen credits is *Bedtime for Bonzo,* a romping satire in which he shared the spotlight with a chimpanzee; Ted Berkman wrote the screenplay.

In reply to the question, "Have you had writer's block?" Ted Berkman said, "Yes," with no hesitation.

"I had wanted to do a medieval Spanish novel, but someone suggested it should be a romantic novel. I gave that some thought, then other things came up. But if I wanted to do the thing, I know I would have done something by now. Still, I have not. I am listening to my gut and it says, Hey, you probably don't want to do this damn thing right now. This is a serious message from inside that is causing this resistance, and maybe I should listen and realize it might not be the greatest project for me."

"But how do you deal with the block?"

"If I encounter resistance, here is an exercise I use. I take a long walk on the beach and take a pad with me, then wait for something to happen. Very often it does.

"If the thing has been rattling around in my unconscious it is very likely to occur when I am moving my body physically, as with a long walk or a swim. Hey, I've written some very good sentences in the water. I memorize them and probably look strange to the people swimming alongside me. They look and wonder and I say something I memorized and they really wonder. I learned to do that at the YMCA in New York, a very good place to work, particularly when I was stuck.

"Sometimes the block occurs out of sheer fatigue, when I have done about all I could do. Then I take a break. Sometimes I go to the piano for half an hour or so and let the thing revolve in my head. I guess I have been a right brain believer all my life. I strongly believe in the workings of the unconscious and keep a pad beside my bed. I find, for me, the most creative time might be when I wake up and before I am fully awake. A sort of amorphous dream state. And before I really fix on the sequence of the day's events, things seem very fluid for me. That's when I grab a holistic-type structure of total concept: *Many writers have said they feel closer to their work at early hours or when they first awaken. Holistic study indicates that we are closest to our conditions of mind, body, and spirit, when we first wake up. The external factors are then least realized."*

"Have you had times when the writing took over?"

"You mean a total immersion into the thing and it goes on its own? Sure. The prime example is Mozart's letter in a book called *Creative Process.* It is fifteen or twenty interviews with creative types. Mozart said he is simply a vehicle through which the whole thing passes. That does not mean to me that he didn't think about it a lot. He probably gave his music a good deal of intellectual thought. Putting the thing down is the final act.

"Ian McClelland Hunter, a motion picture film writer, said most of the writing is done in his head before he writes. The experience for him is a lot like Mozart's.

"I think, with time, one might come closer to that. The novice won't be able to do it, but with a grasp of structure and the process becoming more familiar, it's something akin to driving a car and shifting gears. You know when you are in high, that's when the thing is taking over. There is an interesting parallel there.

"Another feeling with the block is that you have to examine yourself and your own emotionality. Ask, Why am I slowing up? Why is it so difficult? Am I really terrified? Remind yourself that every time the painter faces a canvas the same white paper confronts him as well as the writer."

"Newspaper writers have said there is no such thing as the block."

"Writing a quick journalistic piece about a fire down the block is not the same, other than groping for the right lead."

"Is there a level of concentration the newswriter does not need or realize?"

"Absolutely. There are levels of function. Much of newswriting [Berkman is a columnist for the *Christian Science Monitor*] is a relatively mechanized, left brain operation. You take the pyramid shape, the classical form for a news story which allows the editors to strike out any part of the story without loss of the information. You tell it in such fashion that if everything got knocked out but the top, you could still understand the story. But that's mechanized. You don't need a right brain for that. But you don't write a novel that way. I don't even write a news story that way. The more you develop as a storyteller, the more you are getting into the holistic way of telling a story."*

"Have you even been aware of a spiritual element in your writing at some time in your career?"

---

*This refers to the realization that the fullest extent of one's creative energy comes from the central core of one's being, not from without.

"Do you mean a presence that becomes a guiding force?"

"In other words, did Whistler guide your hand?"

"In one case I can recall, I was writing about Whistler in great length and I began to think of him as Jimmy. His full name was James McNeill Whistler. But I began writing about him as Jimmy all the time. To his buddies, he was Jimmy. But he also became a presence. When I was doing the novel that won the awards, he became almost a collaborator. I never thought of it consciously, but when I sat down to the typewriter it was with him. Jimmy and I went up to McDowell together to finish the book.

"There were no conflicts with him, and I felt great with his presence. I guess to a large extent I became Whistler. I was me but yet like an actor, outside the charcter, a part of it. I suspect, though, that a good novelist like Styron, however much he was visited, would still be consciously directing. You never give yourself over totally to the force guiding you.

"The left brain is doing something like steering. But there will be moments when the right brain takes over and there is no direction at all—it is pure emotionality. You have to learn to ride two horses at the same time. Neither one can dominate, and the right brain horse has to know that when he hits a good stride the other horse will ride along with him. And the left brain horse has to know as well that the right won't run away."

"Have you ever experienced writing something and then finding it was accurate though at first you were not certain?"

"Yes, in a couple of things. I guessed what a person might have done and said and it justified my intuitive knowledge. You must be able to imagine what your character would do or say. I can imagine Whistler twirling his mustache, eyeing some girl behind the counter, and asking her to pose in the nude. Right behind him I can imagine Fanny Holtzman from *Lady and the Law*, looking over the whole place and wondering about doing a sculpture.

"Sometimes talking with good friends will help with severe writer's block, but we all know the danger of that. You don't generally discuss your work. But I have found that calling Gerold Frank or intimate old buddies with whom you can let your hair down helps. Or to walk around the block with them talking and then maybe coming into an idea.

"The final thing of course is that sometimes a psychiatrist helps. I've been in situations when scientists or psychologists were able to point out the resistance. Maybe you don't want to do this and you don't like this guy and no matter how much the publisher says he wants you to do it, inside, you resist.

"Almost everyone I know has been to an analyst for help with this. I mean with writer's block. I am talking about Meyer Levin, after he did *Compulsion* and he had that terrible experience with the Anne Frank diary. He claimed it was stolen from him and that Anne Frank's father got tied up with the Communist party; this paralyzed Meyer's writing for two years. He was in and out of law courts fighting this case. It was only in therapy that he got back on course.

"He had written a version of the play that was true to Anne Frank and he felt strongly that the one on Broadway was a sham and a compromise. He devoted his time and money to litigation.

'I guess so many of these people, by nature of the same sensitivity that enables them to write, find themselves vulnerable. The pores have to be open all the time, but they don't always receive good messages."

William Manchester is adjunct professor of history at Wesleyan University. He has published an enviable list of fiction and nonfiction. His biographies include *American Caesar*, the story of General Douglas MacArthur. *Goodbye Darkness*, an account of World War II in the Pacific theater with the U.S. Marines, became one of the best-selling war stories ever written. Himself a former marine, Manchester is sympathetic with those who suffer writer's block, but is not too threatened himself:

"I do not believe I have ever had a serious block but in 1959 I was in what can only be described as heavy labor. At the time I was writing the last of four serious novels which the critics admired. They predicted a great future for them. They were dead wrong. The customers turned away. The most difficult books to write were *The Death of a President* and *Goodbye Darkness*. They tore me apart. I wept as I wrote."

"What do you do when you labor?"

"In rough passages I use a fountain pen. I write a word in the center of the page. Then I circle it with other words until a pattern appears. That works for me."

"What do you tell other writers?"

"We have a writer's workshop at the university every summer. Young writers come and we discuss problems. I try to discourage them. If they *can* be discouraged, they aren't going to make it anyway. There is a whole cobweb of misunderstandings about writers. In the public view, the writer, unless he achieves fame, lacks the status of doctors, generals, or corporation executives. And no two writers are alike. Even their working habits defy classification. John Hersey is matutinal (a morning person) but Balzac began at midnight. Wolf was nocturnal. I write afternoons."

"Does this mean anyone can become a writer?"

"No. The author belongs to a separate species and may be spotted by his plumage. Perhaps his most striking aspect is his detachment. He is apart from society. 'Writing,' said Hemingway, 'is the loneliness trade.' And the critics are like horseflies; they sting but don't help with the plowing.

"If you describe the life of any writer you are likely to find that he

has already been a man aloof. He may seem jovial but chances are
that this is a facade. He has learned the greeter's smile and winks
the genial wink, laughs the deep-chested laugh, and shakes the
manly handshake because he needs a protective screen. Behind
that screen lives a man within himself, as withdrawn as a
catatonic schizophrenic. The chief difference is that he writes
about it."

"Why?"

"Because despite all circumstantial evidence, he really is sane
and his sanity tells him that no personality is complete without
the understanding of others; that a darkened room is unseen and
the tree falling in the deserted forest cannot in fact be heard."

"Does the writer have a different start?"

"I learned that early fascination with words is a telltale sign of a
child marked for my craft. Reverie is another. Delighted with
fables of Stevenson, Twain, Lewis Carroll, the future author
lapses into glassy-eyed trances and spins a few yarns of his own.
Daydreaming is not confined to novelists. That explains why so
many people say so frequently, 'If only I had time to write.' Or
who actually buy a ream of paper and set to work. We are all
Walter Mittys. I doubt there is a man here who hasn't broken
through the defensive unit of the New York Giants (NFL football
team) at 2 A.M. some sleepless morning."

"And then comes writer's block?"

"Most writers experience the eve-of-battle tension. The chief
reason for it is that the writer knows the battle ahead will be a real
battle and the bloodshed will be his own. It can't be otherwise—
he will be battling himself. E. M. Forster said that a writer dips a
bucket into the subconscious and is amazed at what he dredges
up. Wild things happen over the keyboard at midnight. Peculiar
words come to mind. The writer doesn't even know what they
mean and he may have the Bridie Murphy experience of looking

one up and discovering that although it suits his purposes it passed out of the language a hundred years ago. Talking and quarreling with oneself is an endless strain. The psychoanalytic patient lies on the couch an hour a day for perhaps two years and spends the rest of his time telling his friends what an ordeal it was. The writer undergoes self-analysis forever.

"Others may build a thick floor between the conscious mind and the murk below. The writer cannot. We must peer downward, always trying to make out the dim and ghostly shapes below. Some of them are not agreeable. Aspects of his own personality are unpleasant and sometimes even loathsome. Self-protective instincts intervene. The mind casts a shrouding veil. *The writer has a block.*

"Mark Twain and Joseph Hergesheimer became inarticulate at the heights of their careers and lived out their lives doodling. The fear of running dry is constantly in the back of every artist's mind. Renewed each time he gets stuck. But he goes on groping through the cloaking, soaking fog until he sees the way and the shape and makes the thing right."

"Do you share this with anybody?"

"The late Bernard De Voto once reported that he had discovered a sure-fire way of getting novelists to talk about their work. It consisted, he said, of refraining from speaking for thirty seconds. There are such writers, but I am not one of them. I'm of the breed who believes if you talk about it you lose it. For such a one as I the question: 'What's the new novel about?' is discomfiting. I generally answer that I'm writing a thinly veiled exposé of the questioner."

"Does this mean you want to protect the novel?"

"You must understand that while the novelist is indispensable to the novel, his role is limited. He decides the rules and puts the players on the field. He exercises a certain control. They halt when he blows the whistle and they are subject to his weather. The writer is God and determines climate, temperature, and rainfall. He can even assassinate a troublesome character. But those who remain are not intimidated by him. They are imaginary people but they *are* people with wills of their own, and any one of them can knock the novelist's plot into the wastebasket. The phenomenon of the character coming to life is often treated as a great mystery. It's not really. If the character has been thought-fully conceived, he has certain strong traits and his behavior must be consistent with them. At the outset the writer's people are puppets. Then his Pinocchios come alive. Their wood is now flesh; they move without strings."

"You seem to have very strong feelings about all aspects of writing. Are you that assured yourself?"

"Success (laughing) has not affected me very much because I was forty years old when it happened. I used to be jealous of Norman Mailer because he made it so young. But then it disrupted his whole life. I live a Spartan existence by comparison and don't need much. I make money now, but the spenders are my family, not me."

"What do you do to keep up your confidence and avoid writer's block?"

"One thing I do is play a game whenever I drive long distances. I'll take a year like 1956 and try to remember everything that happened that year—including obscure phone numbers. Once I remembered an old telephone number that took me an hour to recall. But I got it all. Remember, it's all in the memory bank. It's there to get."

Anita Clay Kornfeld is a teacher and a novelist who is as well known for creating an infectious energy in class as building de-nouement in one of her novels. Her best-known works are *In a*

Bluebird's Eye and the novel *Vintage,* which sprawls about the early Napa Valley, where Kornfeld makes her home.

"I'll be happy to make a couple of comments for the chapter on lagging creativity and writer's block, and how I confront the problem," was how Kornfeld began.

"How do you deal with it?"

"I remind myself stubbornly: I am not in competition with any other writer in this wide world other than myself. I must write at my own pace, according to my own abilities, the very best I know how to do, for my very own neurotic reasons. I must believe that what I have to say has a degree of significance, will be somewhere in the ballpark of meaningfulness."

"What do you do next?

"After the pep talk, then I work on the premise that habit creates its own necessity. So let's say I've been on an extended vacation, or caught in some morass of living which has excluded (for whatever other neurotic or healthy reasons) any serious creativity. But I haven't the vaguest idea what will satisfy this itch to write again—except to sit down and try.

"The formula:

"1. Decide how many days a week I will devote to it.

"2. Pick a time of a day and those hours where nothing short of lightning striking me will be allowed to interrupt this interval.

"3. At that same proscribed time, each proscribed day, go to the very same secluded place where there is some kind of surface on which to write. Have tools available: paper, pen, typewriter, and so forth.

"4. I find myself staring at the blank paper, my mind in a blank. I want to go swimming or gazing at the birds. I want to go fix my husband some chicken soup. Or call my daughter. Or play bridge. Or guilt overwhelms me because I haven't written my eighty-two-year-old mother in no telling how long. Never mind. *Sit there*. And start *writing!* No matter what word, what nonsense, verbal gibberish finds its way to the paper, let it spew out, in uninterrupted free association. A curious thing happens. I tell myself, inevitably, I can do better than that. An idea is taking form. I am remembering some rules. Each character belongs to a place and a given time. A character looks a certain special way. Has a name. Has a smell. Weighs how much? Is how old? And before I know it, this character is taking shape! And then I'm asking, 'So where would he or she rather be than here? Or what does he want changed about this particular setting? What's his big problem?'

"5. Time runs out. So the next day, at the same time, pick up where I left off the day before. Free-associate if necessary. But put words down on paper! Try to make them mean something—to take on the happy wings of form and conflict and drama and resolution, double-spaced, with a title and characters who live and breathe, and it will see the light of publication, all things granted."

Charles Schulz is unquestionably America's best-known cartoonist. His *Peanuts* characters have marched into the hearts of American readers and millions abroad. But Schulz paid his dues, working his way up after an army discharge, then returning to school to further his skills. During his career, Charles Schulz has produced and organized a number of films and has participated in writing seminars.

"Are you and Snoopy the same kind of writer?"

"Snoopy and I are two different writers. Snoopy is obviously an amateur, and after thirty-two years I think I can call myself a professional.

"It occurred to me a year or two ago after hearing people talk about writing at writers' conferences and the things that you do about writer's block. This is an amateur's question, because a professional has no time for writer's block."

"What's the difference?"

"An amateur decides that he can't think of anything to write. He worked all day at his first job and he sits down at the typewriter, the easel, or piano, and nothing happens so he walks over and watches TV or goes to a movie—something like that. The professional realizes that he's got to have something in the mail tomorrow, so he does it; that's the difference, I think."

"How can new writers generate that energy the professional seems to have?"

"I sympathize with new people who are trying to write without a contract or without a definite market. To be writing just to throw something out in the wind and hope it's going to sell, having no idea what's going to happen, is very difficult. I went through it all and I know how hard it is."

"How did you deal with it?"

"My key tip for working came from Walter J. Wildwerding, a prominent animal painter. He said that he never let himself be caught without something in the mail. And that became my plan when I was trying to get started. I always had something in the mail. This way you are never without hope. If you have nothing in the mail and you're sitting in your room by yourself trying to think of an idea, you don't have much hope. But even if you have got something out at *The New Yorker,* and you know they're not going to buy it, you have that million-to-one hope."

"Does that mean you send the same stuff all the time?"

"What you have in the mail should always be something different. If you have a short story out then you should have a novel in the mail. Once you've mailed your novel then you should write some articles or a story for *Good Housekeeping* or *Seventeen.* But you should have something out, and that was the best advice I have ever had—an iron in the fire."

"Do you still need motivation?"

"Although I'm never troubled with writer's block, I worry that I'll never come up with a great theme like Snoopy pursuing the Red Baron or Linus and his blanket or Charlie Brown losing all the ball games of Schroeder playing his piano. You know, those broad themes that go so well. I always worry that I'll never think of another one of those and all I will end up doing is grinding out gags, which I don't want to do."

"How do you keep getting ideas?"

"I find that if you stay patient and stay alive, talk to people, do a lot of reading, and stay open, these things will eventually come to you."

"How great does your idea have to be?"

"From around a three- or four-word phrase I'll build an entire Sunday page. Other times I'll hassle the language, work it and rework it, and sometimes never be totally satisfied with the way it comes out."

"Do your Snoopy People give you ideas?"

"I've found about a dozen of my characters provide me with the most ideas. For example, I hate drawing those little birds, especially when Snoopy goes on a hike and I have to draw all five birds. It's very tedious. And I hate drawing Schroeder at the piano with Lucy leaning on it."

"Have your ever tried a novel?"

"I think about a novel all the time but I've never tried it because I don't think I'm a writer. I just don't think I am good enough, so I'll probably never do it."

"Is there a reason for this?"

"Unfortunately, comic strips are looked upon as not being as good as writing, so that's a handicap."

"Would you ask Snoopy for advice to share with other writers?"

Snoopy: "Be very careful how you balance your typewriter on the top of a doghouse so it doesn't slide off."

Saul Bellow expounds on life and philosophy from offices at the University of Chicago, as a member of the Committee on Social Thought. Among his best-known works are *The Adventures of Augie March*, *Herzog*, and the perennial *Henderson the Rain King*, a book of enormous acclaim and recognition.

"I have had my bad times," he said in beginning the interview. "But I never describe them to myself as blocking. It seems to me this is work, or pleasure, that I have freely undertaken, and if it went well I was delighted. But I never thought of it as a form of impotency. When I was younger you went to the analyst to be unblocked, so I could not help but consider it [writing block] as something of the same type."

"What did you feel?"

"First I was miserable and tried to find something else to do, or else changed my topic and maybe blamed it on the manuscript, and wondered if I had chosen a bad topic and should turn to other work. But I can't say I ever described my incapacity to myself as a block—particularly because I thought of it as a harmful description."

"Were some of your books more difficult than others?"

"Some were more difficult. But I had asked for it, hadn't I? And I got into trouble on my own. I found the remedy somehow, I don't know how. But I have abandoned many projects. I didn't abandon a book, though, until I was through and then realized it was awful; that I didn't want to read it myself, so how could I presume to expect it to hold other people's attention? So I spared them as I would have wanted to be spared."

"Was Henderson the Rain King *difficult?"*

"Well, I didn't have difficulty with it, I had difficulty when I was writing it. It was an oppressive time and there was great misery about me. And death was around me too, but I kept writing the book. I turned to it with relief."

"Was it an escape?"

"No, not an escape, I think it was a vacation from everything. The more abuse I was subjected to, the sunnier the book seemed to me. There was a difference in escape and in transcendence."

"Compare Henderson *with one of your later books."*

"Well, the last book compared to *Henderson* . . . mmm, I guess I wrote the last one very fast. But I made some false starts with *Henderson.* But once I got on the track, I ran through it quickly enough."

"What kept you going when you began writing and what do you tell young writers to keep them going?"

"I tell them what a hard life they have chosen for themselves. I tell them I can understand how it is when they face the blank page. The panic. But after all, it isn't that they want only a word of encouragement. But I also know the pain that overcomes the writer when he faces the task of getting something out of nothing. In the early days I felt that panic, but I think it was caused by ambition, not writer's block. I had decided to do great things and found I was incapable of it. After all, who was asking me to do great things?"

"What do you feel now when you sit down to write?"

"I feel like quoting Isadora Duncan to you. When asked why she danced as she did, she said, 'The dance is the explanation. I have no words for this. It involves so much of my life it would be foolish to try and formulate it.' "

"Have you ever felt you were drawing on some spiritual force when you write?"

"I find myself in a state where I feel deeply moved by what I have done. In after thought, I feel it was a spiritual, invisible grace, but at the time I only know that I was terribly worked up over it. If it comes to me in an unnatural form, I put it aside as pretentiousness. If I find myself saying it is some spiritual quality, I say baloney. The way a woman uses her hands or a man pushes back his hair can tell you as much about their spiritual pleasure as any kind of tissue under the spiritual microscope."

"Do you have a favorite bit of advice to offer?"

"I sometimes say to one of my little boys [laughs] that when the wolf comes to the door to hit him on the head with the skillet.

"Just let me tell you one favorite thing of mine regarding writer's block, if you insist on calling it that. About two or three years ago I read the memoirs of Rudyard Kipling, who spent some years in Vermont and built a beautiful house there. One morning a Yankee farmer passed and, seeing Kipling idle on the front porch, said, 'Well, Mr. Kipling, you ain't doing anything this morning.' And Kipling said, 'I don't know anything this morning.' "

Irving Wallace is the Chicago-born product of Williams Institute in Berkeley, California. He wrote and sold his first story for five dollars at age fifteen. Since then he has published fiction and nonfiction, along with hundreds of articles and screenplays, with much success. Of his best-known stories *The Prize*, and its revelations about the Nobel Prize and *The Chapman Report* are continuing favorites.

It would be out of character for a prolific producer like Irving Wallace to have writer's block. This he confirmed:

"As far as I can say, I have never had writer's block. You can't write a book with writer's block."

"What about those parts of a book that are tough sledding?"

"First of all, let's begin with people who have had writer's block. I have found that keeping a journal—not writing to great depths, but covering something of the day—will help. I learned quite by accident that not overwriting has made the creative things more available. My children, Amy Wallace and David Wallechinsky, perhaps by my example have both kept daily journals; as a consequence, the transference of one form to another has led them into writing.

"The whole thing is to put ideas into black and white. I felt that when it came time for them to write books—and I never imagined they would—they would keep right on going. I feel that it comes of the whole idea of having stuff in your head and getting it down. This overcomes a great deal of the fright of writing.

"I kept journals until 1951, when I began doing a daily column."

"How does this apply to your own work?"

"When you get to something tough, like a book I just finished last week, first draft . . . well, I had bad days. I've not formulated this before, but what I do is the night before I'm facing a scene— or sometimes the day before, especially if it's a scene I'm afraid of—I will start making notes in pencil on a scratch pad. I have no pressure there. I can throw them out. And I will start by saying where the logical place for these people to confront each other has to start. And I will put down the logical sequence and then I invariably, by the following day, will have started something in my head."

"What does this accomplish?"

"The next day I will have triggered something. I see it really should have begun in another place, and it all will have happened the night before, things I didn't think of the night before. This gets me going, and another thing, you come right into the scene with a good deal of background woven into it."

"Can you give an example of this?"

"Suppose I have a woman coming into the scene who is a psychologist. I drag out my files and then start making one-liner notes. The notes rather define what Wallace wants from this character, and I get all this down. There are some places where I will skip the factual stuff, as in research, to continue with the imagined stuff. I want to keep the momentum going, and knowing I go back to the factual stuff makes it all right. Sure, there are places where I need more information or more correct information, but I let it go and come back to revise it. Sort of fatten it up somewhat. A lot of writers do that."

"How do you keep track of all this, marginal notes?"

"No, no, what I do is keep rewrite notes. They might say, 'Hey, you forgot to do this for yourself,' and now, when I am done, as I will be Monday on this novel, I will go back and read the notes and plan to revise. I don't read what I have done when I am writing. When I finished I read the novel for the first time. I spend about ten days reading the novel and then make notes. But I don't reread when I am writing. I like for it to come out pretty raw. When I read and make notes on the second revision, I start fixing the holes, writing and rewriting."

"Your system seems to be designed to prevent writer's block more than cure it."

"Maybe that's why I don't like to go to bed with something on my mind. If I have to I will stay up till two or three in the morning fixing things. I'll try to get everything on my mind on paper. Once it is on paper it is safe and I don't have to think about it. I don't want to have a little self-debate when I go to bed."

"Some writers don't have a block with writing, but do have trouble plotting. Could there be such a thing as plot block?"

"Constantly. Most writers I know work with an outline and will sit right down to see what happens—especially with a character. I feel that's death. You might turn up with the wrong novel. What I like to do is have a flexible outline. I might even write five outlines. Some have been as long as sixty pages, single-spaced. And in the final form I break this down into chapters, marking down the logical places for various things to happen. I have always done this and perhaps this does keep me going. But I must say that the writing is not as difficult as the fiction part. A lot of writers I know dread the fiction part."

"You mean the creative part?"

"Right. I remember a novel I wrote that had an ending I was not satisfied with, and I struggled with it off and on until one day, about three months later, lo and behold, it happened by itself. There was a sensational yet believable last and final act. I had to go back and repair some areas due to the change around, but it turned out to be marvelous. I couldn't have been happier."

"Let's shift gears and talk about the spiritual aspects of writing. Are you aware of such a phenomenon?"

"Define spiritual."

"A greater power or outside force that influences your work."

"Not really, except in the sense that there is something mysterious going on. I don't understand, you know? But something happens without your knowledge. I am not religious, although I have finished a book on religion. In respect to spirituality, you have to be open to those things happening. It could be something peculiar to writers."

"Are you saying this something, or force, comes through to writers more than others?"

"There is no question about that. Somehow you wake up and something is there. I can't imagine where it comes from."

John Leggett, Jack to his friends, is recognized as one of the high craftsmen of writing, and thus his position at the University of

Iowa as director of the Writer's Workshop is well deserved. A graduate of Yale, editor for Houghton Mifflin and then for Harper and Row, he was one of the founding members of the Santa Barbara Writers' Conference staff. His biography *Ross and Tom*, captured the tragedies of Ross Lockridge and Thomas Heggen, both young authors who rose to fame and then crashed in self-destruction.

"I don't know that I have writer's block, but I do have a hard time getting started."

"How do you deal with whatever it is you have?"

"I find that the more intimidating thing is the clean sheet of white paper. And if I have a bad hangover or a bad cold and my mind seems filled with oatmeal, I use the back of an old envelope or a dirty scrap of paper for notes. It helps me, and I write my messiest thoughts and get started. Something out of the wastepaper basket this way is not wasted. I am not spoiling a nice piece of paper with my thoughts."

"Has any single book given you more trouble than the others?"

"The one I am working on right now. [laughs] I think like other books, its trouble and pain ends once it is over. Then it's not so bad. But when the work is in progress, it is difficult."

"I know you won't discuss this book, so what was your easiest book?"

"My easiest and most remote was my first book, *Wilder Stone*. I lucked out with *Wilder* I didn't know it was publishable. It became a best-seller and sold here and in England."

"What makes some stories easier than others?"

"I believe that the subject matter has a lot to do with how you are going. When you run out of enthusiasm you do slow down. I did well with *Wilder Stone* because the subject matter basically was my own family origin. An abstract idea can take so long that you lose enthusiasm.

"I take up to five years to do a book. I always think the next book will take a year and at the outside two years. For example, Marilyn Robinson was here and it took her nine years to write her wonderful book, *Housekeeping.*

"If you are not very smart, which I'm not, then it takes longer than you plan to write a book."

"Do you discuss writer's block at the workshop?"

"Students here in the workshop do have writer's block. Maybe it's the competitiveness. One of the ways you get writer's block is you become so critical. Every time you think of something you start crossing it out before you get it on the page. You say, Oh boy that's awful. It stinks. You get very critical and that is self-inhibitive.

"We have a staff psychiatrist here, and she said my problem was that I write with the left side of my brain. She did a study to show the extent writers were schizophrenic."

"Did this study prove anything?"

"Yes, (laughs) it shows that each individual writer differs. I can remember one who said he loved the act of writing. Just sitting down with his pen and going scribble, scribble, made him feel good. That was strange to me, but I think he was sort of one extreme. In fact, any extreme in writing is bad. If you are facile and sit down without thinking very much it comes forth as thin writing. You know, '. . . she's wonderful at writing, but for someone so intelligent and adept she has not succeeded with the novel.' In other words, she didn't reach much depth."

"Is this evident in the workshop writing?"

"In the Writer's Workshop at Iowa City, the people are so winnowed they are already of professional caliber. They know they must become accustomed to discouragement. They don't expect to mail something and have it published. They realize the apprenticeship is ten years, and they accept that. Sometimes they come to me and say, 'I've been here two years and I want you to tell me if you think I am good enough to be a writer.' And I tell them that if you have to ask me, then you don't have it. Don't have the grit for the task. You don't ever ask anybody. If you don't feel it in your anklebones, then you better go sell Toyotas.' "

"Does this mean the surest writers become the most successful?"

"In looking back on students here who have made it and the ones who dropped out of sight. I remember many of the bright ones and they are not heard from, while others who had the energy seem to have made it. A little talent, a lot of intelligence, and a lot of energy is the better combination."

"Who, in your judgment, is the reigning writer today?"

"Once in a while I pick up something. I will probably pick some middle-of-the-road person. If I had to pick someone I would pick an Updike novel. Funny, intelligent."

"What are the things a writer must concentrate on?"

"Most important is to have your own perceptions of real life. Being able to convey that to the reader. I'd say, vision."

Barnaby Conrad, author of more than twenty books, has a list of titles that includes *Dangerfield* and the million-book best-seller, Matador. A graduate of Yale, Conrad is also well known for his portrait painting. After college, he became a secretary to Sinclair Lewis; following this, he actually became a bull fighter, working with one of the immortals, the great Manolete. In 1972 Conrad founded the Santa Barbara Writers' Conference, now considered the finest in America.

"First, I don't have writer's block. The block I do have is in beginning something. If I am working on a story or novel, I write down all the names and characters and what they want. Across from that page I write, perhaps, Jane may want a divorce but Bill doesn't. He wants to keep the family together. The guy who has been pursuing Jane wants Jane—or her money. That sort of thing."

"Why do you do this?"

"It clears the air, and I use the old Hemingway method of going back and rewriting the previous page. Once you get going like that you are Okay."

"What is easiest for you?"

"I like to rewrite. Once it is all down then you've got it trapped. I have never rewritten anything that I didn't believe was improved when I was done."

"What was a difficult book to write?"

"A tough book to write? I'd say that the toughest for me is to have to write somebody else's idea. Like *Fire Below Zero*, which was out of my genre and totally not my idea. *Matador* was easiest. It was written in five weeks."

"Do your books require a lot of research?"

"Some do. I had to do a lot of research for *Keepers of the Secret* [the story of Jesus as a woman] because I had no knowledge of Greek and the basis was archeological information found in Greece."

"Since this one too was someone else's idea, how did you sustain momentum?"

"By the middle of the book things often slow down, but I deal with it by plunging on, even if it means writing badly. You can always go back and correct it. But you must have something on the blank pages."

"What do you recommend for breaking through a block?"

"They say, always have a martini."

"Are fear and tension a factor?"

"Yes, I see a lot of it as fear."

"Some writers are aware of a spiritual influence. Are you one of them?"

"No, but there's a great feeling of well-being when it comes out right. The wierdest thing along that line I can think of happened when I was writing *Keepers of the Secret* and had to pick a name for the female character. I picked, Lael; I had known a woman named Lael and thought it was pretty. Well, about three months later I looked in a book about what to name a baby and there was 'Lael: the chosen of God.' "

"Irving Wallace said writers seem to have a higher awareness of things."

"He's right. I rarely feel anything like spirituality when I am painting. Yet I think of Michelangelo lying up there on his back painting the Sistine Chapel ceilings. He most certainly must have had a sense of spirituality."

"Have you ever had painter's block?"

"Yes, I guess I do—but so much of what I do is on commission and I can't afford to be blocked very long or say 'I don't feel like painting today.' But I do go a long time before I see a picture I really want to paint."

"In regard to writing, would you say there is such a thing as fiction or nonfiction block?"

"Funny you'd ask that. I have never known a fiction writer who couldn't write nonfiction. But there are a lot of writers who can't write fiction. Robert Ruark made the transition and so did

Hemingway. But Herb Caen [columnist for the San Francisco *Chronicle*] had a chance to write a novel about Frank Sinatra and couldn't get past the first page. Herb had never written fiction and yet he does write so gracefully."

Susan Strasberg wrote the book *Bittersweet,* which dealt with her family and provided intimate glimpses of her gifted father, Lee Strasberg, whose Actor's Workshop in New York was internationally famous. A respected actress of stage and film achievements, Susan Strasberg is a teacher and lecturer with an impressive knowledge of right brain systems as applied to writing. During the 1982–83 season she co-hosted the television program World of Books, with Bill Stout, a news commentator.

"Never say 'block,' " Strasberg urges. "Say 'The baby's not born.' My favorite story about writer's block is one with the writer who tapes shut everything in the house. When he writes five pages he untapes the refrigerator. Five more, the coffee pot. And fifteen, the phone. The record player, twenty pages."

"What do you do?"

"For me, I find I get a lot out of meditation and altering consciousnesses. One of the things I am teaching is access to the right side of the brain. I use astrology too, and though it might not be accurate, it works for me.

"About a month ago I had some additional work to do on a book. So I came back and restructured the book and then I came to the creative part and said, I don't feel like it. I had about two hundred and fifty pages left. They needed to be totally re-edited. So, rather than push myself, I did the pick-and-choose work and it was successful."

"You apply astrology to writer's block?"

"I talked to Sydney Omarr [astrologer] about the book and he said it was a very good time for me to do detail work, though not a wonderful time for inspiration. But this time I trusted my own instincts and did fine.

"Several years ago I took a creative journal class and I remember a woman who had a block, not for writing, but a block on life. And they told her she had created the block! It is yours. So when you talk to it, do so as though it were a part of you. I think it helped."

"Does writer's block apply to your life as well?"

"I had this book contract in February and I proceeded to break my leg. My father died and I moved to California. It was like a lot on the karma scale. You know, the death of someone close to you. And moving to California, I started a new relationship as well.

"I couldn't get around it, the book was off timing. But finally I buckled in, and nine months later I got an extension. The book I then proceeded to write was a different book than the one I would have done nine months earlier. But it is much closer to being the book I originally wanted to write."

"Is there some message here?"

"I think so; the nature of the year, the things that happen. How else do we learn? From trauma, pain. I now look back on it all as a graduation. I needed to do this thing on a different level. It was valuable time, just as if you planted a seed and said, 'It's not growing, but lying dormant.' I also think we have rhythms, and people function at different times of day and year. We (humans) are the only living creatures disconnected from those natural rhythms. It takes a lot more work to get in touch with them."

"Are you more in touch with them now?"

"Yes, I told a friend that I don't feel like a writer and she said, 'What do you mean?' And I explained that, well, my working habits are so erratic. Hearing this, she pointed out that I was writing a book a year, that some people took fifteen years to write one book. So I guess it's because I can't write the same hours every day. It bores me and I can't stand it. When I am acting I work long hours, but they are flexible hours. When I write I give myself a block of pages a week. If I do five a day that's fine. If I come to Sunday and I have not done any at all, I do everything that day."

"Other writers use this system too, you know."

"I am not surprised. I think if we looked at it from another perspective we would see the block as an opportunity to either go to some deeper level or realize the block would not be there if there were not something we are keeping from ourself. That block is like an uninterpreted dream. Once you interpret it, the dream may be something you need to know.

"For example, I did not think I was capable of really sitting down alone and doing something like a book. The writing gave me, allowed me, to connect with myself. Opened doors I did not know were there. Writing versus theater."

"What is the difference?"

"The difficulty with writing is that there's no audience there waiting to applaud your work. On the other hand, when you're on stage, you make mistakes and there is no way to correct them. But in writing, you make mistakes and there is always the wastebasket.

"For me, this is a major difference. There are no hundred people in the wings, waiting. My first book, all I had was the publisher waiting. I sold that book on the basis of one hundred pages and an outline. I needed that incentive, I guess, to take time from my other work."

"Irving Wallace says that writers have something mysterious going for them. A spirituality?"

"I don't know that I would call it spirituality, though my whole life is opening up. My publisher said I should eliminate the spiritual transformation I wanted to put in the book. Experiences like altered states, past life memories. And suddenly it was wonderful to be using spirituality and not having to define it while sharing it."

"What if you found yourself stone, cold blocked?"

"It would depend on how close my deadline was. I don't like to write in the morning, but I can write in the afternoon. I mostly like to write at night, when I get a little bit tired and my left brain is a little exhausted. Then the other stuff comes through. I might have to do it with music. I might meditate to create a subjective state in the brain. But at this stage of life I know you are not going for quantity, you go for quality."

"Do you have other measures for de-fanging the block?"

"I give myself choices. Someone told me it was Hemingway who stopped on an unfinished sentence. I guess all those tricks are ways of accessing the creative state. With all the new techniques we don't have to worry. Yet look at all the fine writers who were drinkers, and what were they drinking for? They wanted the left brain to shut up. Yes, there is a part of the left brain that never shuts up—the blabbermouth. Always criticizing, always setting up resistance. I read something Robert Blye said: 'All writers, particularly women, have a little man who sits on their shoulders saying they are not good enough. But all they have to remember is to shut up the little man and keep going.' "

"Do you feel that way?"

"Yes."

"Do you feel inferior to male writers?"

"I feel inferior to most writers. You have to remember I am just beginning. I decided to buy and read everything that was a best-seller. I realized then, after reading that stuff, that the worst thing to happen would be that I will write like this. I have to tell you, that gave me a lot of confidence. There are people who say,

Don't read, it will depress you. I don't feel that way. When I see great performances or read something fine, it doesn't depress me, it inspires me. I reread *Tender Is the Night* and books that have elements of things I remember being very moved by.

"For some reason, most of the books I read about women are written by men. I guess they are writing about what interests them the most. A lot of good women's books are not that popular."

"Do you have reader's block?"

"The hardest part of a book for me is the sitting down. Once I sit down I'm okay, but the getting myself down to do it is the most difficult. The excuses, the things I dream up of having to do urgently."

"How does this differ from writing?"

"You know something, I find the actual process of writing as though I were going on stage. I get icy cold. It is almost a sexual feeling—you know it's all the same. I sometimes begin to shake. I believe that sexuality and creativity and spirituality are the same energy. Maybe the reason a lot of writers have trouble sitting down is they suffer pleasure-anxiety feelings. We have been brought up with these feelings.

"Read Ray Bradbury's article about how he first started writing. It is so beautiful."

"What helps you most in writing?"

"I do a lot of metaphysical things. I have some Indian friends and we do the sweat-lodge thing. There are times when I need a lot of that."

Jack Smith has been a Los Angeles *Times* columnist for twenty years and has published six books. A California native, he was a Marine Corps combat correspondent during World War II. His syndicated "Jack Smith" column reaches a broad national readership, making him one of the best-read daily writers around. This and his knowledge of western ornithology provide his stories with an extensive variety of topics. Jack and his wife, Denny, live in Los Angeles and Baja, Mexico.

"I consider in some ways that writer's block is self-indulgent. I've always had a deadline, and if you don't meet deadlines you don't operate. I write a column five days a week, and I can't call in because I've got writer's block and they say, 'Okay we'll call tomorrow and see how you feel.' And some days the stuff is not very good but you have to say, Here goes, my time is running out.

"I often dig out ideas I've discarded. They weren't good enough the first time, but I dig them out of the trash barrel because the closer the deadline the better they look. It is often an act of desperation."

"Are you sometimes surprised at what comes out?"

"I start a column and after a time I wonder; I didn't know I had those thoughts. It's interesting. I find out that it does take place."

"Do other writers share your views?"

"Some do. I talk at seminars and sometimes run into Ray Bradbury; I guess we're like circuit riders. It was at one of these seminars that I heard Tommy Thompson talk on the first novel he wrote[*Celebrity*], a big novel that he had worked at for a couple of years but he couldn't get started. He had a real case of writer's block—and that same morning I had been saying that writer's block is self-indulgent."

"Were you embarrassed?"

"Momentarily. But I noted too that writers who have had success with their first book and the world is waiting for their second, it seems they have a fear of not being able to do as well."

"Do you think the block is tougher on novelists?"

"I would say that writing a newspaper column or short essay, in terms of writer's block, is fairly easy to deal with. But I've had reporters trying to break in with the Los Angeles *Times*—they panic. One reporter was getting a big feature in and he asked me, 'How do I start?' I think it was the mass of material that intimidated him."

"How do you start?"

"I sit down to write a nine-hundred-word column and have much more material than I need. I get that tight feeling in my stomach, I have so much to deal with. But the best way is to start. Take a paragraph or a quote or something. You know, 'a dark and stormy night.' Anything. But I tell young writers, I know what they are doing. They begin with a clean piece of paper and then start but rip it out. Pretty soon they have a hundred pieces of paper on the floor.

"You get to feeling ill and know you will never be able to do it. But don't do that. Write another paragraph and when you get through and go back to read it you will find that the first paragraph is not as bad as you thought it was. Another trick is to forget the first paragraph and start with the second one. And I said that there are people with deadlines and that makes the difference. But I have to add that that's not altogether true. There are people with books and they have deadlines too and they can't get going. The trick is to start."

"You say start, *but how can you start if you're blocked?"*

"Don't try and win the Pulitzer Prize with the first sentence. I like the low-key beginning. I like to set the stage and get very tired of stuff I read that says, 'A small dark man sat in a doorway and lighted a cigarette, or 'the little old lady was walking down the street with a pack on her back.' I want to know what the story is about."

"What happens with writers battling the block?"

"The most common problem with writers fighting writer's block is diversion. They say, 'Oh, gee, I've got to go up and fix the roof, feed the dog, or mow the lawn.' Other things get priority over your writing. I actually did that once. I went up on the roof to see what kind of view I would have if I put a second story on the house. Or you go get something to eat, or read a book.

"There are probably ten thousand people with as much talent as Norman Mailer, but they don't have his discipline. They can't go into that room and write. The writer who *can* shut that door—shut out wives and husbands, children, movies and television—will win. You have to be a loner during that writing time.

"Fear is also closely associated with writer's block. And again, I have to mention the guy who writes his first novel and it is very successful. He builds a mansion and women are chasing him and he never manages to write another. After ten years he still can't write another."

"Could this happen to you?"

"I have never written a novel. *God and Mr. Gomez* was a collection of my columns that were tied together with a narrative thread. But I do have a signed contract to write a novel. I don't have an advance. But if I did, I'd write it. You see, when I give them an outline, then I get the advance. It's an agreement, but they won't pay me until I give them the outline, and I won't write the outline. So I guess that's my own writer's block. I keep so busy writing columns I don't have time, and I guess I'll keep on. As long as I am busy I don't have to face that novel. I'm not sure I could make up characters and make them believable."

Note: In a later conversation Jack Smith admitted that there is a strong possibility he has novel block. That contract lies in his desk drawer waiting for his retirement. "I plan to work forever," he said.

Budd Schulberg is a Dartmouth graduate; as a student there, he was president of the school's prestigious newspaper. His father was one of Hollywood's most powerful producer-barons. Yet Schulberg has shown throughout his illustrious career one of the most sensitive social consciousnesses of record. His first novel, What Makes Sammy Run, and the acclaim that followed made him the country's most celebrated young writer. But during the Watts riots in Los Angeles he was one of the first to rise to the cause; he founded the Watts Writers' Workshop, which gave black talent a piece of the action. Schulberg's many books are consistently at the forefront of required American literature.

"I'm not troubled with what is commonly known as writer's block. I don't have too many days a week when I feel that I simply can't move. At times I distract myself by trying to do too many things, which is a different kind of writer's block. I'm off covering boxing or doing things, then I look up and a year or two has gone by and I try to do a book every two or three years."

"*Have you had difficult books?*"

"My most difficult book to write was about a Latin revolution, called *Sanctuary V, 1970*, which I started and stopped, moving around trying to find a more congenial spot to work on it. I was so involved in the Watts workshop at the time that I had started the projects stemming from the workshop and was trying to write the book at the same time.

"A book was published from the work in Watts. It is called, *From the Ashes: Voices of Watts*. After that I had to get away, and I went to Florida and Italy, Lake Como, to take two or three months' vacation from the workshop and the book. At the same time it was rather a complicated book with its politics and so forth."

"*Based on your experience with this, what do you tell writers now?*"

"I teach at the Southhampton College and what I suggest about writer's block is that you get into the habit of writing, so if you feel stumped, feel blocked, just write something. Even a letter to a friend or even in a notebook. Even write, 'I can't understand what is making me unable to write today.' At least you are going through the process of putting your fingers on the keys and attempting to write. Sort of forcing your way through it instead of walking around wringing your hands and saying, 'God, I'm blocked.' "

"Some writers credit their fluency with reaching a spiritual level. Are you aware of this?"

"I don't think in terms of spirituality in relation to writing. But I do think of morality. I think if you scratch an honest writer you will find a moralist. I don't think you are in this work, writing, really to entertain the reader or write a page turner. I think you have to write what you believe in and want to convince other people to believe in it too. You are, in a sense, teaching as you are writing."

"What does this mean?"

"It means that writers have to be more responsible than other artists. I've never really believed in art for art's sake. I believe in art for a broader scope for society's sake. I do think that we must think of ourselves as having a special responsibility, whether it's to cry out about an abuse or an attack or defend against nuclear power; we have a special calling, you might say, in that the best American writers must point to what we think is wrong or can be improved."

"You have championed some sensitive issues in your books. What drives you?"

"It comes very naturally to me, and I think you have the best chance to succeed—and I'm not talking about Harold Robbins's kind of success, but in more serious novel writing. I think you have the best chance of actually making success when you take on the project that you are most deeply troubled or concerned about. Those very often are books that do take courage to tackle. Being raised in Hollywood and watching my father, who was not an aggressive man, watching the people around him victimize him with the kind of unscrupulous behavior that would pay off. Writing a novel that would attack that kind of behavior came very naturally to me. When my father read the manuscript *(What Makes Sammy Run?)* he urged me not to publish it because he said I would be ruined in Hollywood and he thought I would need Hollywood to live. He was terribly relieved and pleased when it didn't turn out that way."

"Did that change his feelings about your courage?"

"Yes, even though in some ways it had a negative effect on my father's career. Of course he was at a turning point and was on the way down, after having been very high up there. He was under attack for having allowed me to write such a book. He was proud and glad that his dire predictions did not prove true. For a while, though, I was sort of banished from Hollywood. But by that time the success of the book had opened up all the other writing fields for me. Story writing and such."

"Let's talk about something more recent. In May 1983, there was a newspaper story that reported you asked to have your name removed from the screenplay about Jacobo Timerman, who spent thirty months of torture in an Argentine jail. The article said you were outraged because the producer-director rewrote your finished screenplay. Did this cause a block for you, and how did you deal with it emotionally?"

"I got very upset and kicked the cat. Well, I didn't really kick the cat, it's here on my lap. But this latest episode over the Timerman project—well, it's pretty hard to describe how I dealt with it. The wound is still raw. Especially on a subject that's as timely and significant as this one is to human rights in South America. And to fool around with that is much worse than fooling around with a piece on Prince Charles and Lady Di, or something like that. To mess around with human rights when given the great opportunity to go on a network and say something important is very upsetting to me. I've taken my name off it, but that's kind of a negative victory. In television and film, the writer always has the problem of being rewritten."

"Does this affect all writers?"

"Of course. The writer in the book world used to be more relaxed. When I came into it things were that way, even with advances and money. Now it's becoming more Hollywoodized, though when I first went to Random House as a kid who had just published *Sammy*, it was assumed they would have an obligation to publish everything I wrote. They never questioned it. Now that seems very old-fashioned. If you had an editor like mine, Saxe Commins, he was every bit as good as Max Perkins. In fact, I've republished, revised, and updated a book, *Writers in America*, that might be interesting in terms of this subject.

Note: In *Writers in America*, Budd Schulberg gives an amazing account of himself and F. Scott Fitzgerald wading through the New England snowdrifts, drinking quite a lot, as they both fight writer's block and attempt to convince producer Walter Wanger they are writing a script for *Winter Carnival*, Wanger's pet project. They were both stumped; even more painful is this last look at the faltering lion, Scott Fitzgerald.

Christopher Isherwood has written nine novels, four biographies, and an autobiography. To his credit are a number of plays written with W. H. Auden. Born in England, where he was considered a literary light, Isherwood migrated to Hollywood, where some of his best work was done along with scores of screenplays. He embraced Vedanta, a spiritual philosophy, and became the disciple of Swami Prabhavananda, which inspired one of the most popular and highly discussed Isherwood books, *My Guru and His Disciple*.

"I've had great difficulty and pain with my writing. Once you have taken trouble to write, then you've lost a certain virginity; after that, you can't help but be self-conscious.

"The thought, 'Can I do this, am I up to it, am I doing it right?' these kind of thoughts come to you and then, obviously, the block starts. You may overcome it immediately, but there is usually a hesitation."

"Have screenplays been easier to write?"

"Screenplays are most intricate writing; you are not only writing words, but creating a very delicate pattern. It becomes extremely important to have a correct sense of timing. The timing, the exact arrangement, is very tricky. And of course, you can only do it by trial and error as a rule."

"Your stories are always very candid. Does this take more courage or honesty—or is it just the way your mind works?"

"I don't know if I'd call it courage, but you go on trying and trying to say just what it was all about and gradually, occasionally, you succeed. With all the faults with *My Guru and His Disciple*, it's all unfaked. I sincerely believed everything I was saying, and therefore it was much less difficult than to fake it."

"Can you go into more detail?"

"I only wrote down what I personally experienced, and insofar as the book has any virtue it's a perfectly straightforward account of my relations with this individual, this Hindu monk. I wrote down exactly how I felt, and what he said to me was a matter of record because, especially when we first met, it was written down in my diary and I could rely on it. If writing's worth doing at all it is important to write down as near as you can what happened. Try not to worry about what sort of impression you are creating on other people. I take a lot of trouble with my personal diary; one does it for one's own pleasure, really. You must not ever try to create an impression on a possible reader about how you behaved: Were you being noble, were you scared, were you lying, were you telling the truth? I mean, one must be absolutely frank, and that's not at all easy to do. There are moments in one's life when objectivity becomes extraordinarily important."

"You are somewhat reaching for my next question about owning your own material, not being concerned about how the world reacts."

"I think anything else is a sheer waste of time. Of course, moments must come when you are careful of the danger of showing off. If you are writing about an action you must be careful not to show yourself as being too courageous, or if you are writing about spiritual matters you must be careful not to seem too holy, otherwise a terrible falsity comes. You must be candid—for the reader's sake only."

"Are you applying all this in some spiritual sense?"

"A word like spirituality is very, very loaded. Everybody uses it on different occasions to mean different things. My Guru, Swami P., said quite early in our relationship: 'What you must remember is that to be religious is to tell the truth!' "

"Has this philosophy governed your whole career?"

"Nobody is that honest! But at least you can try to be as close as possible when you are writing something down, so far as religious material, which touches the whole question of, 'Is life worthwhile at all; how are we going to go on living the next day?' "

"Does this openness make writing easier?"

"It's quite hopeless if you are going to lie to the reader about your attitude. Then you are wasting everybody's time, including your own. It's very easy to be insincere, to try and make a good impression on your fellowman, being a nice guy or a courageous guy. Actually, one isn't nice all the time, or at least most people aren't. I know I'm not."

"Did you get much negative reaction from My Guru?*"*

"People are offended by such material from a great variety of standpoints. An account of any kind of religious experience demands the maximum of honesty. It therefore follows that you must not conceal anything about yourself from the reader. Otherwise you are leaving out one of the important factors in the situation. It may invalidate the whole thing. Quite a lot of people who otherwise wished me well found it in very poor taste that a book which was supposed to be beautiful and spiritual introduced the fact that I am homosexual. This shocked them and they thought it had no bearing on the subject. Nothing could have been falser. Ramakrishna [a Hindu holy man] himself said that everyone must come to God as he is: A thief must come to God as a thief."

"Did you later regret such honesty?"

"I would be shocked if any kind of spiritual teacher took an ethical stand about a person by saying, 'If he does this or that he's no good.' That means the teacher is not worthy to be a teacher. Swami was quite unshockable by what his devotees shared with him, and some of them were exceedingly frank. He sometimes had an almost despairing laugh, but he never judged—except he would be very disturbed by things that had to do with untruthfulness. Swami Vivekananda [a legendary Vedanta teacher] said you can live with anyone and forgive anyone but a liar. Then it becomes unmanageable. The very foundation of the situation is false. How can you believe anything they say? How can you help them or how can they get better?"

"Was your writing affected by the negative reactions to your book?"

"Well, very often, of course, people are very tactless because they don't have the know-how to express themselves in a courteous manner, and then perhaps you are not in a good mood that morning and react or get angry or whatever. But I don't see any other possibilities than being truthful no matter what people think."

"What would you tell the new writers?"

"I would tell all beginning writers: Look, if you really want to be a writer, that is great. But it really is a very, very serious undertaking. And if you are prepared, that is fine. But don't feel you have to do it for any other reason but that you want to do it.

"There is a whole question that has to do with ethics and art. But it's impossible to do in one conversation. I'm getting on. I'm seventy-nine now."

Fannie Flagg is an actress and author whose first book, *Coming Attractions*, is as funny to tell about as it is to read. Flagg was a writer for Allen Funt's *Candid Camera* television show for several years. She lives in Santa Barbara, California, dividing herself between publishing her next book and performing.

"I have had the worst case of writer's block since my first book and I cannot get started. The first book I wrote was done when I had no idea how to write a book. Know what I mean? And then when I started I realized what I was getting into. And I said, Oh, my God."

"What did you do?"

"I have done things to keep from writing, like having my entire mouth capped. That means I have to go to the dentist and can't write. Then I decided to move. That would keep me busy. I really liked where I was living, but moving kept me from writing."

"Why do you fight it?"

"I have all these ideas but I don't know where to start. I find that I like to talk about my ideas and the minute I do then I don't have to write about them. And I will talk to everybody. The real estate agent. The plumber. Anyone who will listen."

"Was it that way with your first book?"

"The first book was funny, but it was not all funny. Some people told me, 'You know, I liked your book, but I think you are capable of much better things.' They have no idea that it's hard to write comedy."

"Is this your greatest problem?"

"No, I have trouble with two careers. I am also an actor, and when I think about writing I wonder about my acting. And when I am acting I worry about my writing. Then I have people who tell me, 'How can you write when you are such a good actress?' Others say, 'What are you doing acting when you can write so well?' It's affected me to such an extent I am neither fish nor fowl."

"What is your background?"

"I started writing when I was a kid. I used to write little sketches and everybody would love them. When I was older I did some writing and came to the attention of Allen Funt and went on to work for *Candid Camera* for about five years. That kind of writing was very much off the top of your head, and I had not given much thought to serious writing. Then in 1976 I came to Santa Barbara and saw an ad on a telephone pole that said the Santa Barbara Writers' Conference would have Miss Eudora Welty coming. I went and signed up for the whole thing, not knowing that I didn't have to do that to hear Eudora Welty speak. And then they had a writing contest at the conference and I wrote a short sketch and won the first prize."

"Did your writing career take off?"

"I was terrified. I had always wanted to write, but decided the next year, Oh well, I am not going again, that was just a fluke. And

I didn't go to the conference the next year, but the year after that I decided that, well, maybe I'll try it again. And then I won the first prize again. This time I decided, uh oh, maybe I had better try this.

"I had a friend who knew an editor and sent my stories to him. The editor called and said he wanted to see me in New York. He wanted me to write a book. I said, 'Oh boy, I'll be just like Eudora Welty and have a book of short stories." But when I went to see him and said that I could come up with more short stories, he said, 'I'm not interested in short stories. I want a novel.'

" 'My God,' I said. 'I don't know how to write a novel. How long is a novel?' And he said, 'About four hundred pages.' "

"There is no need to ask if you went for it."

"They gave me a contract and some up-front money, so I went home to write this novel. I decided to weigh four hundred pages to see how much paper it would take, and it came to about two pounds and some ounces. After that I would write, then weigh my day's production to see how I was coming along. When I got to the right weight I knew I was at the end of the story. I was lucky because when my story ended I had about four hundred pages."

"Was the publisher satisfied?"

"It was a nice book with no sex or violence. It didn't sell much, but it was the most rewarding thing in my life for a long time. Now I'm stuck. I don't know where to go from here. Everybody says write more of the same, but I don't know. If I write more about my character I'd have to take her into television and I don't want to do that. I'd like to write a murder mystery that takes place in the 1930s, but my publisher says they don't sell."

"What advice can you give to writers with a block?"

"If I were telling someone else how to break through their writer's block I would say to get in there and sit for an hour or so even if you don't put anything down. You have to develop the discipline to go in there every morning."

"If doing this is so easy, why are you fighting it?"

"Because I had more personal satisfaction from writing that book than anything I've done. In my work there has never been a finished product. When a show is done the curtain comes down and it's over with. But to walk around with something tangible— it's wonderful. And the residual effects are wonderful too. And the people I have met are wonderful.

"How have you kept your enthusiasm with writer's block hampering your production?"

"When the book was done I was down for a while. But then the postman came with a box of letters from people who had read the book. They were relating to me as a person and not as a personality. They were touched in a way I had never touched anyone before. In acting you use somebody else's words, but these people were touched by *my* words. It was a whole new way of life, and I began to look at myself in a different way."

Art Buchwald is a writer who requires little introduction. His syndicated column is a staple in America and abroad. To his credit are a stage play and several books. But his flair for political satire is unequaled, and for those who have endured his barbs, Buchwald is the first to say that he is in no danger of running dry. Ever.

"We are not allowed to have writer's block in the newspaper business. Writer's block is for people who don't have deadlines."

"Do your columns come that easily?"

"Sometimes they come fast and sometimes they don't. But I gotta get them in. So I am never allowed the luxury of writer's block. I don't mind if the column takes off and writes itself. A lot of columns do that and take a flow of their own after I start out with an idea. Maybe in the middle of it I have to stop and say, Wait a minute, that's not the idea."

"During the Nixon era you wrote some of your best columns. Can you tell why this happened?"

"Sure. There was so much to work with. You had Watergate. And Nixon, you could always depend on him for ideas. It was a great period. I'd vote to have them all back again. Nixon, Haldeman, Ehrlichman, the whole gang, the whole group. I sure would."

"Does this mean that Reagan's administration is dull?"

"No, he is good copy for column writing. He is doing a lot, making changes in a lot of things. I would give him an A on a scale of ten."

"Why would you give Reagan an A?"

"What would I give him good marks for? Well, first of all, he keeps getting his facts wrong. That is really helpful for a column like mine. And the changes he's made give me something to write about. Most of all, he had people like James Watt, which is gold to columnists like me. I used to say, 'I hope he never lets Watt go.' "

"Do you feel like sometimes you get a little spiritual help from somewhere?"

"Yes, I assume there is somebody upstairs helping me, particularly on a dull day. I don't question gifts. I am not a mystic. I just accept creative gifts."

"What about the column you are facing right now?"

"I am doing one about the CIA director, William Casey. He was playing the stock market during the time he was CIA director. That brings up the interesting idea that the guy in charge of intelligence is able to know about what to invest in at the stock market. This column will write itself."

"Is a lot of your success due to your feel for dialogue?"

"Sure, I am comfortable with it. I like conversation and I just feel good about dialogue. People like to read it. You write an editorial piece and there's no quotation marks. A bit of dialogue always helps."

"What advice do you have for struggling writers?"

"I have no advice to tell anybody. I don't know what to tell anybody. I get that request a lot, but I have nothing to say except if you are getting in the newspaper business then forget about writer's block. You don't take no for an answer or you don't take rejections and you think that everybody else is an asshole but you."

Alex Haley is the author of two books, one of which had a profound effect on publishing. That book was *Roots*, which documented the tracing of Haley's ancestry from slavery in this country to Africa, where his Mandinka origins are as old as the land. A second, *Autobiography of Malcolm X*, has been regarded as one of the few exact accounts of the American Muslim movement. If ever a writer had to write his way out of obscurity to fame, Alex Haley is that writer.

"I heard one of the most eloquent descriptions of writer's block several years ago at the Santa Barbara Writers' Conference. This was before you wrote Roots *and you told about owing thousands of dollars for research expenses. You weren't able to write and you told of crossing the Atlantic in the hold of a freighter to search out the feelings of thousands of slaves who also came that way. You could hear the slaves as you lay there in the dark and felt like stepping off the fantail into the sea. How did you shed this feeling to write?"*

"The depression absolutely was there. I never thought of it as writer's block; it was kind of circumstantial—a low point. I have always interpreted writer's block, from what I've heard, as something where you simply find yourself unable to get on with it. You just sit and stare at the page and, in a sense, I feel that is writer's block. I have always felt myself blessed that I have never experienced something like the block."

"Do you have a writing problem?"

"Yes, my big problem since *Roots* has been trying to find the time to write the way I used to write. At the time I was on that ship I wasn't really involved in writing, I was researching. But when I get to the writing part, I am truly blessed. Give me the clear time, immersion time, and I can get almost high off writing. It's euphoric."

"What is that like?"

"I get tunnel vision about what I'm doing, and I tend to average anywhere from two to three times my normal output. I'm an incurable rewriter. I might rewrite from five to eight times on almost everything."

"Doesn't that much rewrite cause you an enormous amount of work?"

"Right now I'm making some large changes. I have always felt inhibited by word processors—I'm so used to the typewriter. But almost every major writer I know tells me I am a fool if I don't make the transition."

"You travel so much, Alex. Could that be a means of escaping? Avoiding the writing?"

"We all do that unless we get into what I was talking about—the creative euphoria. I regard with impatience the necessity of even going to the bathroom when I'm really into my writing. But when you are on the periphery, trying to get into writing, you find all kinds of reasons to get up and do this, that, or the other."

"What would you tell beginning writers?"

"The beginning writer has no legitimate reason to say he has writer's block; he's not a writer yet."

"I take this to mean it's doubly tough without credits. So how did you do it?"

"For the beginning writer it's like looking into a maze, a mist, or a fog, not knowing which way to go. His block is something else entirely. I was always fascinated with the intrigue of writing, and when I was a sailor (I was a cook) I would finish the dishes and look forward to writing after I had taken a shower and then a nap. About the time everyone else was going to sleep I was going to my typewriter to write for two or three hours each night before I slept. That became a habit with me. I love writing at sea. It helps me to write every day."

"Is this one of the things you want to change in your life?"

"If I could organize my life as I would ideally like it, I would spend one month at sea and one month ashore, alternating around the year. That way I would get my maximum output because I would write at sea and do all the other things I need to do when I was ashore. I've got almost too many subjects to write about. I keep coming back to being obviously blessed, especially when I hear about what other people go through."

"A number of the writers I talked to mention a spiritual element or awareness when they write. Are you aware of this?"

"I live on the spiritual element. Again, when I go back to the euphoria I mentioned, it's absolutely spiritual. It's a force I feel that is with me in a way I don't understand; I simply accept it. It's just something that happens, like for days I will just feel cloaked and I'm turning out pages like magic. I especially felt this when I was writing that part in *Roots* where Kunta is in his village as a boy, and certainly parts of the book when he was in the slave ship crossing the ocean. I tend to find that when the research has been intense, the writing will also be intense.

"Another spiritual experience would be when Kunta was first in this country and he was set into a cultural conflict—this was a kind of high moment to write."

"You mention research—do you always research as intensively as you did for Roots?"

"Generally, I spend so much time and effort in research I have probably overresearched. I rarely use two thirds of the material I've gathered. I like to feel I know what I'm writing about."

"Have any of your books been easy to write?"

"I've only written two books, and neither of them was easy. *The Autobiography of Malcolm X* and *Roots* were not easy, nor would any book be if it was a good book."

"Why do you continue to push yourself to write when your life and time are so intensely in demand?"

"I love my work. I love to write. One of the biggest problems beginning writers have is that they don't appreciate how much work goes into being a professional writer. Writing looks easy to people who don't write. *The better the writing the easier it looks.* But writing is hard. It is so easy for a beginner to think that he can write because he writes good letters or he got good grades in composition or his aunt says what he writes is great. Most people say, If I write two months or six months—and some are generous enough to say a year—some magazine or book publisher might accept my stuff. That's utterly farfetched. My view is that it takes about as much time to become a professional writer as it does to become a surgeon. You have so many people entering writing—I would compare it to someone with first-aid capability applying for acceptance as a surgeon.

"Beginning writers must appreciate the prerequisites if they hope to become writers. You pay your dues—which takes years."

Artie Shaw is a glamorous name associated with the big band music of America's swing era, a man whose many marriages to some of the most beautiful and exciting women of the time have almost eclipsed his brilliant career in music—but not quite. And now Shaw, the man, is writing. He has published books and continues to write and lecture on how it is done. In Oxnard, California, he taught a class for the college program. In Santa Barbara he participates in the writers' conference. His home is in Thousand Oaks.

"Artie, you have written books and written music. Is there such a thing as music block as compared to writer's block?"

"I don't think so. I believe that music flows a little better. It comes easier than with a book. You see, a book can be read. You hand it to somebody and they can read it. But hand them some music and they can't—music doesn't come to life until it is played."

"Can you give an example of that?"

"Okay, take for example Chopin. The notes of music he wrote are only a convenient form of notation. People who play those notes as they are written will only have a stereotype and not capture the real feeling he intended in improvisation. I write music that way to allow the musician to interpret in his own style. But it's not so with writing [prose], which is one of the purest forms of communication."

"Have you ever known a blocked writer?"

"Matter of fact, I once helped a friend remove his writer's block. You know the famous writer Robert Lewis Taylor? His book, *The Travels of Jamie McPheeters* won a Pulitzer and became a Disney film—a young boy traveling down the Everglades. Remember that story?

"Anyway, Bob came to me one day, he's very macho. A big strong, male kind of guy—almost too much. He always believed in the sock to the jaw and talked a lot about the blood-red soil of southern Illinois, where he came from.

"Bob knew I'd been in analysis, but he liked me anyway. I knew as much about hunting and fishing as he did. He wrote me up in *New Yorker* and we went fishing a time or so and he forgave me the psychoanalysis. Felt it was too probing."

"What happened?"

"Well, he came over one day, pacing up and down, and finally he said, 'I don't know what the hell is going on, but I can't write. I guess you could call it a block.'

" 'What happens?' I asked. And he said, 'Well, I go to where I work up there by the tennis court and I can't write.' So right away I tell him, 'I know, you walk up and down and sharpen a lot of pencils.'

" 'Nothing' comes,' he said.

"Then he tells me he's really worried. 'I'm not getting my twenty pages a day.' Hearing this I said, 'Hell, that's a funny amount. How come twenty and not ten or forty-eight?' And then I told him that I had an idea. Why didn't he do what was in his control. Just sit in the chair for four or five hours, however long he worked, and just write what he could. So he went back and about three days later he called and said, 'Hey, Artie, it worked. I am writing again, and in fact, I am getting my twenty pages a day.' "

"All he had to do was break the rhythm to regain the rhythm?"

"Right. Like making a curbwise leap into another concept. Now he thinks I am about the brightest guy on earth. But most writers don't realize that it's like writing a bunch of letters. You put the good parts together and you got a book. If not a book, then a short story."

"Have you ever had writer's block?"

"Hey, I don't go into that kind of thing. The only thing I've had is occasional times when I did not see any point in continuing. For example, I started a book that might end up being a trilogy. By the time the guy is twenty-three years old in this story I got 1,250 pages, so I know I am not going to get him to age fifty very soon. It is going to be a longish book, right? And I got to the place where I thought I had better go rethink my position. I gave myself one year off."

"Was writing music that way for you?"

"No, I had an audience. With books I don't write for an audience; I write for myself. I was talking to a group called the Santa Barbara Screen Writers' Association and I told them that I was writing a book for which I got up in the morning and worked several hours, then stopped. I do not care if anyone ever reads it, I told them. I am writing it for myself. And one of the guys got up and said, 'You are very lucky to be in that position.' So I told him, 'I worked forty years to be in that position. I can tell you about this thing called luck. I worked like a dog to get that position.' Luck?"

"Speaking of luck and writing, have you ever been tempted to write a book about your life and romances back then when you were being chased by all those bobby-soxers?"

"I can honestly say I turned down thousands of dollars years ago to write about all that. I don't believe in it. When you are married and have personal knowledge and shared experiences, it's not right to publicize it. I don't know, I just feel that way. It's not honorable and I never will write one of those [bleep]-and-tell books."

"You could write a best-seller?"

"I don't care. I don't believe in that sort of thing, although there is an idea I've had for some time, and that's to interview people all over the country with successful marriages. That would be a great book, I'd think. You know, how do they do it and so forth."

"In another direction, Artie, have you ever been aware of a spiritual or 'other' presence when you work?"

"Not so much in those terms. You might say I have had this happen: When you come into that rhythm, seven days a week, four hours a day, when the typing comes automatically. I usually end in the middle of a sentence and write the last page so fast that it will have a lot of errors and mistakes. I can't wait to get back at it the next day to clean it up."

"What does this do?"

"Every once in a while, say I've written seventeen pages, I will wonder; Where in hell did this come from? I have no recollection of writing this. And I find that this is some of the best stuff I write. And that might be what you are talking about when you say 'other' presence. It's like going into a stranger's mind, something you are not aware of."

"Does this ever happen in music?"

"Oh hell, yes. In Carpinteria recently I had a notion that I had to write a tune. Then I did a draft of it and added a few bars here and a couple of measures there and it was a hell of a nice song. Roger Kelloway, great pianist, played it for me the other day and it was good. It was one helluva tune. I hadn't written one in fifteen years.

"My girlfriend plays flute and she was playing and then she stopped. Right then this tune popped out. But it's not luck. They say luck comes to the prepared mind. I believe that."

Margaret Millar is the Canadian-born author of over twenty books. She is a University of Toronto graduate and was the 1965 Los Angeles *Times*' "Woman of the Year." An enthusiastic birder and nature lover, Maggie Millar wrote one of her few nonfiction books, *The Birds and the Beasts*, then returned to her first love, fiction. Though she is legally blind with a retina dysfunction, Millar continues to write, and until recently, to regularly tend as well to her famous husband, Kenneth Millar (Ross Macdonald), who was tragically stricken with Alzheimer's disease (see Note, page 204).

"My writing is coming very well, thanks."

"Have you ever had writer's block?"

"I say no, I've never had writer's block, but I am being troubled but that is different. I see no connection. Usually for me it's a matter of plot or I've been on the wrong track. When this is the case all you have to do is do something about it."

"Have you always been so sure of your writing?"

"I've retired a couple of times, but I always unretire because I have the habit. But I think this thing about creativity is strange. As soon as I finish a book or I compose a poem I make up a song on the piano and it's always the thing that keeps on going. It touches every part of my life because I don't do things the way other people do them."

"Have you thought much about how some books come so much easier than others?"

"Certainly. Sometimes I get a first-class idea and carry it all the way through. That makes it a tour de force. I think, *Ask For Me Tomorrow* was one I carried all the way through. That was quite a tour de force. That kind of book had a lot in it that was difficult."

"What's your system?"

"I keep enough notes ahead of time to learn which of my characters are going to carry all the way through and which are not. Say I write fifty pages, then I find which ones are going to last and which are dull and ought to be dropped. You have to do this or else you end up writing about someone who was only a minor character."

"How would you describe your books?"

"I don't think my books have any heros or heroines. I like to avoid that."

"How would you describe your nature book?"

"It was a pleasure, but the research was difficult. I was very insecure and I can't understand how I had enough nerve to start writing a book about birds when I had only been observing them for four years. I had to study real hard. This was a fact book, and I don't like to stick to the facts. I am a fictioneer, as you say. I will never write another fact book, I guess. I am a natural-born liar or fictioneer."

"What if I were a beginner and asked you what to do for my writing block?"

"I'd say don't come to me, kid. I got problems of my own. And I get a chance to say that about once a week. Ken was always the teacher and critic. He enjoyed helping people. And I do too. I'll help them across the road and help them with their animals, but I'll be damned if I'll help them with their writing because I don't feel I have it in me."

"Did Ken ever have writer's block?"

"That blabbermouth? No, no, he never did. He considered writing a real privilege. That is how he always acted. He worked for years without taking a holiday. We thought people were crazy, talking about a holiday when they were doing the greatest thing on earth."

"Do you think Ken was free of the block because he paced himself? You know, he always worked for about three hours a day writing in longhand using a board on his lap."

"Yes, that's right. But when he had the urge he would write longer. But when you want to make it a steady thing you have to pace yourself."

"What keeps you so vigorous, keeps you writing?"

"I'm able to swim a half mile every day of my life and I don't try and show off, but try and pace myself. Another thing, if you had to live by writing, I'd say you pretty well have to have both people in it and you both have to write very hard."

"You mean husband and wife?"

"If you are going to make a living at it, yes. If one of us was doing books, we understood. Once in a while we were both finished at the same time and that was great. Usually, we were between books."

"Did you help each other?"

"I was never able to exchange editing with Ken, but I did when he started his first two books. I always thought that when he was writing and I was reading along with him that he could not write dialogue. He was writing everybody as if they were speaking the same way he was. And I take credit for one thing, because I really think I taught Ken to write dialogue."

"Do you feel strongly about dialogue?"

"My ambition is to write a book so that when people read it and hear one sentence, they will know which character is speaking. That, to me, would be great. Dialogue is my forte and I like people to talk the way I think they should talk."

"Do you listen to people when you are out?"

"I am a terrible eavesdropper. You are not safe having me around when you are talking."

"You mean like eavesdropping in elevators and restaurants?"

"Every restaurant and elevator I have been in. I listen in on everything I can. There's some very interesting things around— oftentimes some very personal conversations. And if you think I don't listen to them you're nuts. Once I was out with Ken and he said to me, 'I'll bet you can tell me what everyone in the restaurant said but me.' "

"*Some writers believe writing embodies a certain spiritual element. Do you?*"

"Are you kidding? No, no, I should say not. I am not very spiritual. I am a realist."

"*Have you ever been writing and guessed at something to later find it was right?*"

"Yes, but I probably knew it or remembered it from some other time."

"*Can you explain why writing has come so easily for you?*"

"Ken and I both had a very strong Canadian education. And with a background like that you don't have to wonder too much if you are punctuating right or not. You know damn well you are. And I am sorry that we are getting away from that. Now when I go to court that we are getting away from that. Now when I go to court and listen to some of the lawyers speak, whatever God-knows-what tongue they are using, I begin to concentrate on their errors and redundancies and I stop listening to what they are saying. I actually find myself correcting their language. I got a transcript now of a trial and my heart went out to the court reporter because they have to record everything the way it is spoken. And if someone says, 'I ain't goin' to do nothin' no more' then the reporter has to put it down that way. Even if it is a lawyer saying it."

"*Do you capture that in your stories?*"

"No, I try and clean up their profession and protect them as much as possible. I might need a lawyer someday. I have a notion that if any of them heard me say that—well, who can say?

"But there was one lawyer who never used bad grammar. He

helped me a lot when I needed a point of law. He was careful, but not too many lawyers are anymore. You know some of the lingo, 'What's comin' down?' and that sort of thing. They certainly don't take enough English in law courses."

"Would you say this is a problem with writers?"

"Of course. Illiteracy? Yes, indeed. You see they have gone too far the other way with it. It is not too readable."

"Why is mystery writing your favorite genre?"

"I prefer to write mysteries because, within certain limits, you can say what you have to say: life, love, and the pursuit of happiness. All you need is a bit of framework."

"If Ken had been able, what might he have said lately to writers about writer's block?"

"Oh, good Lord, how would I know? I never could predict what he was about to say. Diana Cooper Clark, one of the heads of department at the University of Toronto, interviewed us. It must have been about four years ago. She had interviews with several writers when she lived here and I remember getting a little profane at one part and I hope she left a few things out. People tend to ask the same question and I have a tendency to say, 'Bullshit.' And when I get a tendency, boy, I express it."

"Margaret, I don't have to tell you that Ken had many friends or how much we miss him, do I?"

"Yes, I miss him too. What I miss mainly is that we talked so much together. We had common backgrounds. We had so many points of reference. I could start a poem and he could finish it. You know, that kind of thing. When he was ill, oh, those times I went to see him and talk to him, he couldn't hear and he didn't turn his head and he just was not there. He was a dead man and was still walking around. I didn't feel sorry for him, he was not in pain and he was not depressed. I mean, I am so glad he did not have what his father had—a stroke—and his father had to live five years without being able to talk, yet being aware of everything. I would prefer this fact for Ken rather than have had him in pain. He didn't know what was happening. He did not know where he was."

"He would be proud of you, soldiering on and writing in the old tradition."

"I know he'd be proud of me, he always was. And that's a nice feeling. But if I couldn't write—oh boy!"

Note: Kenneth Millar (Ross Macdonald) died July 11, 1983, in a Santa Barbara, California, convalescent hospital. His contributions to writing and the mystery genre were widely lauded. In 1973 the late Robert Kirsch, Los Angeles *Times* book critic, said: "Macdonald should not be limited in audience to connoisseurs of mystery fiction. He is one of the handful of writers in the genre whose worth and quality surpass the limitations of the form."

Ken and Maggie Millar both grew up in Canada and were married more than forty years.

CONCLUSION

Every human creature has creative capacity. Some have greater access to that capacity than others and seem to accomplish impressive bodies of work with lesser natural abilities. How do they manage this? Mostly with faith and trust in their inner forces.

Successful writers have these same deep convictions along with a firm grasp of their creative energies. They have learned that neither education, nor opportunity, nor accommodation combined can equal the accomplishments of those who write with confidence and trust in their own creativity. Every chapter in this book is written with this in mind.

Guidelines, instructions, and suggestions are helpful but nothing works as well as the determination and belief you invest in your writing—regardless of the opinions of others. For this reason the weak writer who pushes ahead with confidence will become stronger by writing and rewriting, over and over.

"It's like a radium seed of irrevocable desire in my gut," a beginning writer said ten years ago. Today that writer is teaching writing. This same seed exists in each of us, dormant in some, but glowing persistently in others. And here is the further intent of this book: to fan alive that seed whose inner flames will only be quenched by creative expression—writing.

Too many of us are writing for the wrong reasons: to sell, to please, to gain power. All are secondary. We must first write to satisfy ourselves, to cool that inner burning. Writing in its purest form is subjective, the result of our feelings and perceptions. Writing is right brain, the essence of self-expression. Believe this, practice it, and incredible worlds await. Write on!

INDEX

Aaron, Hank, 5
Access, right brain, 56, 63
  easy, 56
  limited, 14
Action substitute, 88
Actor's Workshop, 171
Adams, James L., 65
Adversity, 52
Alcoholics, writers, 99
Alsop, Stewart, 110
American Plains Indians, 10, 113
Annadar, 67
Atman, 109
Auden, W. H. (Isherwood), 182
Avid-reader, 75

Background, 122
"Basic Sweat Lodge," 11
Bedtime for Bonzo, 147
Beginning, 94, 95, 103
Beginning, stronger, 123
Beginning writers, 52, 186, 193
  pay dues, 194
Bergman, Ingmar, 39
Bernstein, Carl, 50
Black Viking (Downey), 70
(Bleep) and tell books, 197
Block:
  astrology, 171
  hitter's, 4
  novel, 178
  painter's, 4, 70
  plot, 4, 164,
  plumber's, 147
  reader's, 175
  sculptor's, 4
  writer's (see Writer's block)
Body, 107, 110–111, 117, 148
Bogart, Humphrey, 96
Boredom, 23, 26
Bradbury, Ray, 13, 68, 176
Bradley, Mayor Tom, 140
Brain shift, 3
Brainstorming, 47
Brown, Charlie (Schulz), 159
Browning, Robert, 89
Buck Rogers, 17

Caen, Herb, 171
Caldwell, Erskine, 83
Capote, Truman, 105
Carver, George Washington, 5
Center for Democratic Institutions, 71
Centered individual, 112
Characterization, 44–46, 122
  and chemistry, 48
Characters, 155, 199
Chopin, 195
Clark, Diana Cooper, 203
Columbus, Christopher, 51
Comfort, 52
Commins, Saxe, 182
Confidence, 44
Confinement, solitary, 23
Conflict, 57
  information, interest, and revelation, 93, 94
Conversation, helpful, 138
Conviction, 130
Cooke, Alistair, 147
Corpus callosum, 13
Creating from right brain, 74
Creative:
  energy, 61, 175
  groove, 42
  inner forces, 48
  people, 11
  quotient (CQ), 16
  saline-tank emersion, 11
Creativity, 36–37, 40
  cutting edge, 66
  the elephant, 37, 38
  on own terms, 37
  pause, 29
  trust, 37
Criticism:
  advice, suggestions, 43
Curiosity, 94

Da Vinci, Leonardo, 17
Dead man, 203
Deadline, 76
Des Moines Register and Tribune, 22
  (see also Miller, Frank)
Dialogue, 201
  (Buchwald), 191

Didion, Joan, 25, 105, 146
Dirksen, Senator Everett, 93
Discharge, 138
Dolphin fish (mai-mai), 36
Don'ts, 10
    early, 32
Dot, 100, 101, 104
Draft, 82
    first, second, third, 82
Dreams, 3
Drivel, 29
Duncan, Isadora, 161
Dunne, John Gregory, 146
    (see also Didion, Joan)
Durant, Will and Ariel, 139

Eavesdropper, 210
Edison, Thomas, 8
Editing, 73–91
Editing refinement, 74, 77
    pencil, 8, 124
Editor:
    desk, 78
    his ear, 79
    publisher's mind, 32
    villainous, 78
Edwards, Betty, 14, 56
Ehrlichman, John, 190
    (see also Nixon, Richard)
Eisenhower, General Dwight D., 6
Endings, 124
English, grammar, 15, 74, 202
Energy:
    exterior, 119
    inner, 108
    spiritual, 48, 117, 119
Erving, Julius, 21
Exercise:
    breathing, 115
    handwriting, 67
    (see also Writing exercises)
Extrapolation, 46, 47

Father writers, 9
Faulkner, William, 105
Fictioneer, 200
First-page impact, 90, 124
Fitzgerald, F. Scott, 82
Forster, E. M., 153
Franklin, Benjamin, 8
Funt, Allen, 186, 187

Gardner, Ava, 96
Gibbons, Euell, 16
Gunning, Robert, 86

Haldeman, Bud, 190
Haley, Alex, 146
Hemingway, Ernest, 4, 15, 82, 169

Hemispheres, divided, 13
Hercules, twelve labors of, 3
Heresheimer, Joseph, 154
Hersey, John, 152
High purpose, 118
Higher self, 112
Holism, 107
Holistic, 6
    balance, 116
    condition, 113
    existence, 114
    harmony, 118, 119
    power, 147
    study, 148
    way, 149
Holistic state, functional, 108
Holtzman, Fanny, 150
Homosexual, 185
Hunter, Ian McClelland, 149
Hutchins, Robert, 71

Idea file, 49, 71, 72, 126
    unused material, 142
Ideas, 71–72, 159, 163
    from God, 71
Illiteracy, 203
Image words, 60–61
Imagination, 31, 51
    double dip, 46
Indian worship, 10
Information:
    gaps, 139
    research, 47
I-me, 109
Inner feelings, 33
Inner resources, 122
Inner world:
    explore, 112
Inner writer, 42
    always on, 52
    breaks rules, 64
    private, 39
Inspiration, 125
Inspirational blackout, 29
Intelligence quotient (IQ), 16
Interviewing, 140

James, Henry, 4
Jones, James, 83
Journal of American Indian Education, 113

King, B. B., 140
Kipling, Rudyard, 162
Kirsch, Robert, 14, 204
Knowing, 32
Krantz, Judith, 146

Ladd, Alan, 96
Lael (chosen of God), 170
L'Amour, Louis, 20
Lardner, Ring, 83

Left brain, 3–6
  activity, 27
  blabbermouth, 174
  formula, 36
  left brain—right brain, 66
  limitations, 114
  now, 17
  steering, 150
  terms, 11
  thinking, 102
"Lefthanded thinking," 6
Levin, Meyer (*Diary of Anne Frank*), 151
Little novels, 123
Love Your Librarian Day, 143
Luck, 197

Macdonald, Ross, 198, 204
Mailer, Norman, 146, 155, 178
Mandinka, 191
Marginal notes, 81
Marijuana, 11
Michelangelo, 40, 170
Michener, James, 135
Middle, 123
Millar, Kenneth, 198, 204
Millar, Margaret (Maggie), 204
Miller, Frank, 22
Mind, 107, 111, 117, 148
  game, 32
Mitty, Walter, 127, 153
Money—left brain, 52
Moore, Robert Hamilton, 97
Mother writers, 9

Nixon, Richard, 190
Notes—keeping ahead, 199

O'Brien, Tom, 12
"Off the Wall," 63–66
Omarr, Sydney, 171
Outer writer (public), 38
Outline, 80–81, 92, 94
  first-page, 96
  flexible, 165

Patton, General George, 6, 8
Peanuts (Schulz), 157
People watchers, 52
Perfect first pages, 82
Perkins, Max, 83, 86, 182
Philadelphia 76ers, 21
"Pippa Passes," 89
Plimpton, George, 146
Plot, 49, 122, 164
  plot, left brain plan, 49
Popular Mechanics (magazine), 141
Pornography, 53
Prabhavananda, Swami, 182
Professional writer, 194

Quinn, Jim, 89

Radium seed, 206
Rama, Swami, 111
Ramakrishna, 185
Rawproduct, 33
Reaching within, 114
Read, 96, 97
Reader's mind, 32
Reagan, Ronald, 147
Red Baron, 159
Rejection, 84
Research:
  believability, 135
  finale, 141
  intense, 194
  story blend, 142
Rexroth, Kenneth, 79, 103
Rewrite notes, 164
Rewriting—again, again, 125
Rhythm—every day, 198
Right brain, 6
  anxiety, 8
  exercises, 5–11, 14, 22–25, 26, 28, 31, 43, 47,
    57–58, 60–72, 108–109, 115
  expression, 7
  few rules, 98
  fugitive, 17
  holistic, 98
  identity, 56
  interference, 56
  related forces, 48
  sensation, 58
  shift, 9, 20
  to start, 97
  storytelling, 96
  thinking, 12
  trust, 37
  what-if, 51
  (*see also* What-if)
Right hemisphere, 4
  (*see also* Right brain)
Right mode, 125
  (*see also* Right brain)
Rules, 123

Safe crackers, 30
Santa Barbara Screenwriters Association, 197
Santa Barbara Writers Conference, 68, 85, 143,
  166, 168, 187, 191
Schaefer, John (Shane), 95
Schools and technology, 6
Screenplays, 183
Scribner's, 83
Seasoning, 33, 126
Seduction, 96
Self-discovery, 133
Sexuality and creativity, 175
Shift, the, 24
Shifters, moderate, 21–22
Shifting right, 25

Show, not tell, 43
Simple sentence, 59
Sinatra, Frank, 171
Skills, adversary, 76
Slow producers, 33
Smith, Jack, 84
Snoopy (Schulz), 157, 160
Spirit, 117, 148
Spiritual:
    element, 193
    energy, 117, 119
    experience, 194
    influence, 170
    peace, 118
Spirituality, 165
    both hemispheres, 18
    morality, 180
    very loaded, 184
Stein, Gertrude, 83
Stenography, 4
Stone, Irving, 146
Storytelling—an excuse, 131
Styron, William, 46, 150
Survival kit, 7, 108
Sweat lodges, 10

Tanks, saline, 11
Taylor, Robert Lewis, 195
Think, 29–30
Thinking, 4
Thompson, Tommy, 51, 176
Thousand Oaks, 195
Tibetan monk's prayer, 110
Timmerman, Jacobo, 181
Tom Bass, 44, 46
Tour de force, 199
Trust:
    instincts, 102–103, 107, 109, 110
    writing, 47
Tunnel vision, 192
Twain, Mark, 154
Typing, 4

University of Iowa Writers Workshop, 166, 167
University of Toronto, 198, 203
Unrelated statements, 61

Validation, 111
"Vases and Faces," 57, 58
    (see also Writing exercises)

Vedanta, 182
Verbs, action, 88
"Visions Through Fasting—Intermediate and
    Advanced," 11
Vivekananda, Swami, 185
Voice:
    active, 88
    passive, 88

Wallace, Amy, 163
Wallechinsky, David, 163
Watergate, 190
Watt, James, 190
Watts Writers Workshop, 179
Welty, Eudora, 105, 146, 187
Wesleyan University, 151
What-if, 30, 49
    listed, 32
    negative, 31
    working, 31
What-iffing, 140
Whistler, James McNeil (Jimmy), 147, 150
Wilderwerding, Walter J., 158
World of Books (Strasberg and Stout), 171
Wolfe, Thomas, 82, 83
Woodward, Bob, 50
World War II, 17
Writer's block, 2–5, 14, 29, 62, 66, 110, 147–148,
    155–158, 163, 166, 167, 171–174, 176–178,
    179, 182, 183, 186, 188–189, 195–197, 198
    after first book, 186
    demon, 9
Writer's Workshop, 167
Writers as consumers, 8
Writers Market, 85
Writing:
    effectively, 135
    exercises, 123–133
    (see also Right brain exercises)
    groove, 57
    Hemingway, 152
    horned demon, 14
    listen to, 87
    mind, 32
    music, 197
    mystery, 203
    at sea, 193
    style, 88
Write on!, 206